The Heartbreak Handbook

THE
Heartbreak Handbook

Valerie
Frankel
and
Ellen
Tien

FAWCETT / COLUMBINE · NEW YORK

Sale of this book without a front cover may be unauthorized. If this book is coverless, it may have been reported to the publisher as "unsold or destroyed" and neither the author nor the publisher may have received payment for it.

A Fawcett Columbine Book
Published by Ballantine Books
Copyright © 1993 by Valerie Frankel and Ellen Tien

All rights reserved under International and Pan-American Copyright Conventions.

http://www.randomhouse.com

Published in the United States by Ballantine Books, a division of Random House, Inc., New York, and simultaneously in Canada by Random House of Canada Limited, Toronto.

LIBRARY OF CONGRESS CATALOG CARD NUMBER: 93-90029

ISBN: 0-449-90757-0

Designed by Fritz Metsch

Cover design by Bonnie Timmons

Manufactured in the United States of America
First Edition: January 1994
10 9 8 7 6

To all the women
who lived to tell

Contents

Acknowledgments

THANKS TO Julia, Chi, and Anita Tien, and Judy, Howie, Alison, and Jonathan Frankel for getting us here; our editor, Julie Merberg, and our agent, Loretta Fidel, for all their help; Howard Blaustein, Colette Dartnall, Manny Howard, Judy McGuire, Carol Rosenbloom, Joel Tractenberg, and Jacquie Wasser for all the obvious reasons; Kim France for the worst 24 hours of her life; Marshall Sella (or as he is known to millions, "Morsel") for his funny, funny editing skills; Frank Rosenberg for helping us meet Will and Glenn; and Will Dana and Glenn Rosenberg for helping us be so frank.

And special thanks to all our sources (we know who you are).

The Heartbreak Handbook

1

The Beginning
of the End

ALL GOOD things come to an end. Relationships are no exception. Don't get us wrong, we're not trying to be nega-holics; it's just that every relationship is really a series of phases—as each phase concludes, you (hopefully) find your-self at the beginning of a new, better one. Some relationships progress from the dating phase to the every-weekend phase to the deeply committed phase, steaming right on ahead to the monogamy phase and then, oh, maybe the living-together phase, culminating in, what the hell, the never-ending love/ joy/eternal bliss phase. But you don't need a handbook to advise you on how to struggle through a lifetime of happiness. As such, the phase we're going to talk about is . . . phase out.

In other words, The End. But don't touch that Kleenex— yet. Even ends have their beginnings. Every devastating breakup (a redundant phrase, if you ask us) has its warning signs. Usually, we women, intuitive, sensitive, all-knowing creatures that we are, can spot trouble, swift like the wind. And how. Our deep self-awareness, that pesky gift, can tune us in to all manner of weird relationship vibes. And although denial often afflicts the best of us, eventually, when the blinders come off—and they do come off—we are forced to recognize that all along, there were red flags a-flying. Hence, the refrain: *I should have seen it coming.*

Like snowflakes, no two breakups are exactly the same. But again like snowflakes, all breakups, despite differences in size, shape, or detail, pretty much leave you cold, damp, and sniffly and can make it tough to leave the house. In short, although each romantic catastrophe may seem unique, there are always common denominators within the genre. And with a little help from one or two (hundred) of our heartbroken friends as well as some bona fide heartbreak therapists, we've deduced that there are five basic travelers' advisories that can clue you into rough weather ahead. So before you buy him another expensive birthday present—read this:

1. The Distancing Technique (or, Keep Away)

When it comes to breakups, the distancing technique is the number-one signal of impending doom. According to Dr. Judith Sills, a Philadelphia psychotherapist and author of *A Fine Romance*, distancing involves one member of the relationship investing less of himself or herself in the other person. "If he's the one doing it," says Dr. Sills, "you'll notice him withdrawing both emotionally and in terms of time and attention. Distancing is the most common symptom of a relationship's end because it's the easiest to do. Most of the time, men leave a relationship in order to find or be with someone else. By pulling away, he can start to make room in his life for that someone else."

It's a pretty elementary technique, but as someone once said

(we think it was Lord Byron, but maybe it was Warren Beatty):
In simplicity lies great and treacherous power.

Take Val, for instance. She and Mark had been going out for
a year. Everything was just peachy until . . .

VAL: The Valentine's Day Massacre.

ELLEN: What do you mean by that?

V: Well, I had been telling Mark I was in love with him for a
couple of months. He wouldn't say it back, but I tried not
to push him. Even though he didn't respond, I kept saying
it; it became my mission to make him say it back.

E: Always a sign that a relationship will flourish and grow . . .

V: Shut up. Anyway, on Valentine's Day, I got him a present,
I wrote our initials in lipstick on the mirror, I cooked dinner,
I (sigh) created a loving environment.

E: Uh-huh.

V: We were all set to watch *The Princess Bride* on television—
it was a special holiday presentation—and I thought that
seeing the movie on top of all my efforts would make him
utter those magical words to me, for sure. I said to him, "I
love you, I want you to tell me you love me."

E: No way.

V: Way. But he didn't. He said, "I can't say that and not be
lying. I'm very attached to you, but I don't love you." I cried
all night. We had sex anyway. I don't think either one of us
enjoyed it; I know I didn't. And from there on in, the
warning signs kept on flowing and I just kept holding on.

E: The other warning signs being . . . ?

V: He would make plans that didn't include me. I would call all
the time and he would be busy. He never talked to me about
his life; he never told me what he was doing. When we did
see each other—at my urging—he was distant, he would
barely participate in conversation. Basically, he gave me just
enough to keep the relationship hobbling along, but no

more than that. Then, I started to get afraid, probably because I knew the end was near. I was apologizing constantly for everything; once I spilled a drink and apologized for an hour. Literally. I couldn't stop saying I was sorry until he told me to put a lid on it. Sex petered out. What sex we had was soulless. It was dead.

E: Harsh.

V: I'll say.

The warning signs in Val's and Whatshisname's relationship were pretty classic: Whatshisname became unavailable, emotionally and sexually. But you don't have to be living in the same city with a guy to get distanced by him. Linda, twenty-seven, was in a long-distance relationship with Marvin, for two years. After about a year and a half, it suddenly became even longer-distance:

"He took a job in upstate New York, and I stayed in Manhattan. In the beginning, things were great: We talked on the phone a couple of times a day, we saw each other every weekend. It was sexually charged, romantic, exciting. But then the calls began to dwindle from a few times a day to once every few days. He said, 'When we don't talk for a while, it gives me a chance to really appreciate you.' I didn't like the sound of that.

"When I met Marvin, he was a virgin and had never been in a serious relationship before. I felt like I had broken the ice for him sexually and emotionally—and suddenly I was hearing a certain cockiness in his voice. Still, I didn't think he'd be shopping for other women because we were so much in love. He finally called and said that he thought we should see other people. I said fine; I thought he just needed to say that and he wouldn't really carry through with it. How could he? I mean, he loved me.

"The weird period continued. Our phone conversations

were plodding and perfunctory. But he would always give me a thread to hold on to. 'Bear with me,' he'd say, 'I haven't been myself.' He was always careful to tell me that he loved me. But it didn't sound particularly genuine. The last straw was when my grandfather was having surgery. I needed his support, and he was nowhere to be found."

Yep, pretty classic. Don't think that the warning signals are always male-instigated, though. In the case of Nancy, twenty-eight, a photographer in Seattle, the initial breakup noises came from her. And although she suffered her share of heart-ache after she and her boyfriend, Wayne, made their split, she definitely was the one who put the machine into motion.

"I had been going out with Wayne for two years. I knew the relationship wasn't my final frontier, but he was so good-looking, so charming. I went out with him for vanity, for sex. I think I held myself back emotionally because I knew that I could never trust him. Flirting was like a lifetime hobby for him; he wouldn't be satisfied until he had dated every woman on earth.

"We drove cross-country together, and after that, something in me shifted. I started to look for a job in another city. This took about three months. I was planning to make a new life for myself, but I never even told him about it. Somehow, subconsciously, I was trying to create a world that didn't include him. I didn't do it on purpose, but now I see that it was the only way I could bring myself to make a clean break from him.

"During those last three months, I came to depend on him less. Everything that used to bug me didn't bug me anymore. I'm almost sure he had a fling with someone during that time, but I didn't even care. At that point, I couldn't be bothered to get angry. When you can't get really angry with someone, you know that the relationship's over."

. . .

Sad, but true. What have we learned from these three stories? In a nutshell:

THE DISTANCING TECHNIQUE
How it works: One member of your relationship (for the sake of not getting crazy over nonsexist pronouns, let's just say it's the guy) makes himself unavailable. He doesn't write, he doesn't call—you get the picture. **How it makes you feel:** Frantic. The more aloof he is, the more desperate you are to *make him love you.* As always, you badly want what you can't have. **Overriding emotions:** Guilt (you're convinced that it's your fault that he can barely bridge the gap between ape and man). Despair. **How you should react:** You should try to divest yourself of the situation, make yourself independent. According to Dr. Sills, the best thing you can do is back off— if he's feeling trapped or choked, this will ease the tension. Besides which, if he's pulling away, he'll only be more annoyed and run away even faster if you glom yourself all over him. **How you do react:** You glom yourself all over him. **The upside:** Now you have plenty of time to reacquaint yourself with all the friends you blew off when you started going out with . . . Him.

2. The Change Factor (or, Making Mr. Right)

"When I first met Matt," says Penelope, a thirty-one-year-old investment banker in L.A., "he had just quit his job at an advertising agency. For the next six months, he worked in radio, public relations, marketing, television—he used to joke that he was the ultimate Renaissance man. He was so random, so undirected, especially compared to me, the ultimate stress-for-success woman. At first I thought he just hadn't found anything that interested him yet. I figured I could help focus him, give him a nudge in the right direction. I don't know, *I guess I always thought he would change.*"

Pardon us, do we hear a dirge? Fact: If you spend a lot of time in your relationship wishing your boyfriend will change, be careful what you wish for. Because odds are, he *will* change — girlfriends.

We know that there's no such thing as perfect male-female compatibility. If you envision yourself as Ms. Yin looking for Mr. Yang, even if you're of Asian descent, we suggest you rethink your romantic strategies. True, in the first flush of love, the fact that he's never on time for anything or that he throws his dirty socks in the oven or that he clips his toenails in bed may seem . . . endearing. But when the rose-colored glasses lose their tint, you may (or may not) find yourself with irreconcilable differences.

Keep in mind that just because he says tomato and you say tomahto, you don't have to call the whole thing off. In every good relationship, there's a certain amount of c-c-c-compromise. And luckily, different people have different pet peeves, so both parties rarely have to undergo total overhauls (for example, to Val, a toenail or two in the sheets would be no big deal — she's not squeamish; she'd just brush them onto the floor — but dirty socks in any room where there's food would be a relationship buster. Ellen, on the other hand, doesn't even like having contact with her own toenails but probably wouldn't notice the socks since she never uses the oven anyway). Basically, it's all about you and your honey trying wholeheartedly to curb your behavior and, at the same time, extend your tolerance levels. It's about accommodating each other. It's about (Maestro, *Sesame Street* theme, please): cooperation.

But what if he refuses to cooperate? Or what if the problem

isn't quite as simple as toenails and dirty socks? What if he's cheap (you hate cheap) or sarcastic (you hate sarcastic) or insensitive (boy, do you ever hate insensitive)? And what if you find yourself relentlessly and, yes, annoyingly, trying to give him a personality makeover? Well, then, we've got news for you—and it ain't good. "Part of being in a relationship is acceptance and understanding," says Dr. Sills. "If you can't live with him the way he is, then maybe you shouldn't be with him in the first place."

Don't believe us? Consider the fact that Penelope and Matt dragged on for a year and then broke up—true to form, he still didn't have a steady job. Or look at Rachel, twenty-nine, who learned three years, two carats, and one bad relationship later that some things never change.

"I met Nick three years out of college. We hit it off immediately—he was so witty and charming, we had so much fun together—and fell in love fast. He was from a real Waspy family in Connecticut. He got sent to prep school when he was very young. His father is the head of a big ad agency; his mother needlepoints. They're Republicans. Need I say more? I thought it might bother them that I was this liberal, Jewish girl from New York (and sure enough, it did), but Nick kept saying to hell with them, he loved me.

"The problem was, his father had a real hold on him. He was incredibly cold, demanding, critical. All the kids lived to please their father; the whole family used to sit at his feet while he watched television, they always went on vacation together. Nick and I never were able to go away alone, we always had to be with 'the clan.' Once, we went with his family to Japan for two weeks and we never had a second to ourselves. I kept asking Nick if we could at least have one dinner à deux, but he was too afraid to say anything. I kept hoping he'd take a stand, but he never did. Still, I figured that maybe it was enough that

I had been invited in the first place—and that things would get better later.

"We had been going out for about two years when Nick proposed to me. Shortly after that, he took a job in Chicago, and so I left Columbia grad school and transferred to the University of Chicago to be with him. When we moved in together, things started getting shaky. His parents called at all hours of the day. He started working late. I became a flaming nag. We fought constantly. But we chalked it up to the stress of our new life and continued on.

"I knew there was going to be trouble when I set the wedding date. Nick didn't check the date with his father, but he said that he was sure it would be okay. It wasn't. His father made us try to change it, but we couldn't. Then, one weekend, I went to New York to go to Bergdorf's with my mother to buy my bridesmaids' dresses; Nick went to Connecticut to see his family. When we got back to Chicago, he told me he had talked to his parents—and that now he was unsure about getting married. Later, I found out his parents had said, 'She's not one of us, she never will be, we want you to call it off.' A month later, he did.

"Now, when I look back, I realize that throughout the entire time we were together, I had hoped that Nick would be able to overcome his parents' dominance of his life. I thought if he loved me enough, he would stand up to his family. Not a chance. Ultimately, he had to make a choice; I don't know why I was surprised that he would choose to be his parents' son rather than my husband."

Ouch. The moral here: Don't think that a year or two of love can suddenly reform a lifetime of habit. But wait, there's more. The tricky thing about the Change Factor is that the source of conflict isn't necessarily an issue as concrete as job motivation or family influence. It can be something that creeps up on you, something that maybe wasn't there in the beginning of your relationship, something intangible and hard to put your finger on, like, say . . .

ELLEN: Depression. Gloom. Misery.

VAL: Would you like to elaborate on that?

E: Not particularly.

V: Well, try.

E: Okay. Let's see. Jake and I went out almost four years. For the first two years, we had a really great time — we did fun things, we never fought, we gave each other a lot of space. It was so right. We used to say how lucky we were that we found each other.

V: Sounds pretty grotesque. Go on.

E: Well, around our two-year anniversary, his work schedule (he was in medical school) became incredibly grueling; he was exhausted all the time. On the rare moments when he wasn't working or sleeping, he was cranky as hell. At first, I attributed it to his sleep deprivation; I mean, I'd be cranky too if I had to work like that. But then, even when his hours improved, his mood didn't. He got more and more depressed. But he refused to talk about it, with me, with anyone.

V: So what did you do?

E: I didn't know what to do. He was a whole different person, he had become . . .

V: His evil twin.

E: Exactly. I started spending less time with him. We went on separate vacations. He became testier and more difficult; I became unaccommodating, sarcastic. We started fighting all the time. I began to suggest that we see other people. But I kept thinking, if he could just snap out of his depression, if he could just change back, everything would be perfect again. It dragged on this way for about a year. Then, one day, I remember turning to him and saying, "You know what? I just had a huge revelation—that just about everything is more fun without you."

v: Shit.

e: That's what he said. I apologized—but deep down, I really meant it. And at that moment, I realized that no matter how much we loved each other, the situation was never going to change. Jake wasn't going through a phase; this was just the way he was. With me, at least. And all the love in the world wasn't going to make things any different.

v: Brutal.

e: I'll say.

In other words, Making Mr. Right might be a cute title for a movie, but it has no bearing on reality. Penelope, Rachel, and Ellen all found that out the hard way. Their experiences with The Change Factor (as well as those of scores of other women) can be summarized as follows:

THE CHANGE FACTOR
How it works:
As your relationship progresses, you find yourself saying with increasing frequency, "Things will really be perfect as soon as he stops doing *(put your gripe here)*." **How it makes you feel:** Cheated, dissatisfied, driven—you know that your life could be ideal if only he would change this *one small thing*, and so you're going to make him change it, dammit, if it's the last thing you do. **Overriding emotions:** Irritation (because he isn't changing), confusion (why the hell isn't he changing?), despair (he'll never change, will he?), resignation (no, never). **How you should react:** After a short period of nagging, you need to search deep within yourself and make a personal choice: You either resolve to live with *(your gripe)* and get off his back, already; or you move on gracefully. **How you do**

react: You nag, you whine, you sob, you hang on for dear life—you do everything except move on gracefully. **The upside:** Eventually, you realize that you are not omnipotent, that you cannot control and change other people, nor should you try. You see that what works for you does not necessarily work for everyone. This is called becoming emotionally evolved. As an extra, added bonus, you are absolved of being responsible for anyone else's shortcomings and thus can concentrate on fine-tuning your own.

3. The Fight Report (or, Love Is a Battlefield)

No love (or no love worth having, anyway) is totally smooth sailing. That would be ridiculous, and boring, besides. True love calls for a little tussling, a little (in Val's case) hysterical scene-making, a little (in Ellen's case) verbal jai-alai. When he puts the empty Chinese food carton back in the fridge or flips television channels like his life depends on it, of course you're supposed to carp a bit. When you take an hour getting dressed or you send him out on too many tampon runs, of course he's entitled to complain. But if you find yourself regularly crossing the line from friendly skirmish to drawn battle, what should you do? In two words: Watch out.

"There's a healthy stage that every relationship reaches where both people take off their masks, acknowledge differences, and negotiate a middle ground," says Dr. Sills. "When you can move toward a resolution, then fighting is productive. But when the fights become mean, unfounded, and there's no release of tension, then you're in dangerous territory. And if you're just picking fights in order to get close afterward, well, then you need to ask yourself whether you're in the relationship that's right for you."

Since different people have different fight styles, it would be bootless to say that any one brand of altercation points to relationship disaster. After all, one couple's bloody melee may well be another couple's five-minute squabble. What's more, the actual fighting, per se, is not necessarily a surefire sign that the love is gone. For example, one couple we know of — let's call them the Bickersons — slammed doors and shrieked at each other on a weekly basis. But, despite public prediction that the relationship would crash and burn any minute, to everyone's surprise the Bickersons got married. And stayed married. It turned out that all the screaming and melodrama was merely the (highly unorthodox) way in which they communicated; the high decibel levels were not an indication that the relationship was doomed.

What *is* important to look out for is a significant change in the fighting. Are the two of you fighting with increasing frequency and/or hostility? Are you saying things you wish had gone unsaid? Are the fireworks louder and more dramatic than ever before? Are they sullen, unresolved, lingering? Do they make you feel worse instead of better? If so, says Dr. Sills, you'd be well advised to take cover.

Nina, thirty, a lawyer in San Francisco, says she knew that things were taking a turn — for the worse — in the fourth year of her five-year relationship with Stephen, a fellow attorney.

"We met in law school, in the spring of '86, and moved in together after we graduated. It was a pretty healthy relationship. Sure, we bickered off and on, but our arguments were about little things: who was going to water the plants; did we have to have dinner with my mother, again; why couldn't he put his dishes in the sink instead of leaving them on the table.

"Then in the summer of 1990, he took a job at the law firm where I worked. Jobs were scarce; it was a good offer, and we figured that as two mature, rational adults, we could iron out any of the stresses that working together might present. We didn't tell anyone we were involved; we didn't think it would be a problem. And in the beginning, it really wasn't. It was fun to have him in the office, to eat lunch with him, to discuss cases and dish our co-workers with each other at night.

"Gradually, though, the fun ended and tension kicked in. It all began when a paralegal who had been working on one of Stephen's cases asked to be transferred to one of mine. Stephen was really ticked off; he felt like he had been slighted—by the paralegal, by the partner who let her switch, by me. After that, things started to get weird and competitive. We started to fight—a lot. He started to pick apart my work, belittle me; in response, I got hostile and obnoxious. Our fighting went from a minor blow-out once every month or so, to an all-day, everyday, tense undercurrent. And whereas we used to fight about silly, nitpicky stuff, now we were harping on these huge, global, unresolvable issues. He started to make these nasty remarks about my intelligence. I made innuendoes about his questionable work ethics, his poor management skills. I think that for a year, we really . . . despised each other.

"It got uglier and uglier. We completely avoided each other in the office. When we were at home, we never talked like human beings; we either raged at each other or sat and smoldered in separate rooms. When we had sex, it was edgy, almost animalistic, wired with anger.

"We said things to each other that year that could never be taken back. I remember sitting in the bedroom one day after a particularly vicious exchange and thinking nothing can heal these wounds. Nothing. Obviously, he thought the same thing. The next weekend, I went to stay with my mother in Redondo Beach; when I came back, Stephen was gone. He had moved all his stuff out to San Diego, where—without ever telling me—he had gotten a job. I sat in the apartment and felt kind of lost, not having someone there to rail at. The whole fiasco wasn't anyone's fault. We just got so caught up in our war; it devoured our relationship and became bigger than the both of us."

For Nina and Stephen, the romance didn't die until sniper fire had escalated to deadly levels. For Tamara, a twenty-five-year-old Berkeley grad student, it was a totally different kind of shift in fight style—a downshift—that signaled the end.

"About two and a half years after we started going out, we stopped fighting, almost entirely. Which may sound too good to be true, but in our case it was a bad sign, since our relationship thrived—maybe even depended on—healthy, daily arguments. We were able to talk things out and fix them by arguing—the fights were heated but good-natured. I don't know, it was like we needed to exercise our lungs or something.

"The downshift occurred around the time we started talking about where the relationship was going—were we going to move in together, would we get married, and so on. Up until then, it had been a fairly relaxed, "what happens, happens" sort of arrangement. By trying to cement things, both of us suddenly became ambivalent. We were scared. I guess we realized that we weren't sure that we wanted to spend the rest of our lives together. As a reaction, we started being really polite to each other, not talking that much—and never, ever fighting.

"It was awful, all that politeness. We broke up amicably a few months later. We realized it wasn't going to be the ultimate relationship. After being together for so long, it was hard to give it all up, but I knew when the shouting stopped, when we didn't love each other enough to disagree with each other, that it was just a matter of time."

Granted, Tamara's story (particularly the part about breaking up amicably) is an unusual one. However, it handily illustrates the fact that it's not *that* you fight, it's *how* you fight (and, more important, how your fighting changes) that's significant.

That said, it's time now for a wrap-up:

THE FIGHT REPORT:
How it works: You and your loved one find yourself battling it out in ways you never dreamed you would. **How it makes you feel:** Like you want to knock his block off. Or, another possible alternative: Like you want to knock his block off, but you can't be bothered. **Overriding emotions:** Anger, hostility, resentment, and a certain scary, yet exhilarating, lack of control. The worse it gets, the less control you have. **How you should react:** For starters, take a deep breath and count to ten. Thousand. **How you do react:** How does an eight-hundred-pound, insanely angry gorilla react? Any way it wants. **The upside:** Incredible catharsis. Plus, in the midst of a fray, sometimes you're so cruel and clever you scare even yourself—and this prevents you from lashing out at really important people, like your friends or your boss or your mother. Well, maybe not your mother.

4. Commitment Lust (or, Love Me Do)

Loving unions are all about giving and taking, making and meeting requests. There are so many small things that each person can ask of and do for the other to make the love grow. For example, Val's request to be told, at least once a week, that she is breathtakingly beautiful has done wonders for her partnership. Ellen's request that she be told, at least twice a week, that she is more beautiful than Val has done likewise. And since your partner can't be expected to read your mind, the premise here is: Ask and ye shall receive.

But hound, and ye shall end up with . . . jack. If you autocratically require your sweetie to do anything, odds are he'll demur. Again, the principle of reverse desire (what you want, you can't have) applies, but this time, with a twist: What you demand him to do, he won't. With a vengeance. With piddling day-to-day conflicts, this dilemma can be resolved by . . . giving up. As someone once said (we think it was Krishnamurti, but maybe it was Bonnie Raitt): Release the desire and it will be yours. If you suck it up (nudge, nudge), bite the bullet (wink, wink), and give him a break, he'll probably give you one, too.

But suppose your piddling demands become, well, un-piddling. Suppose they escalate way up, from one dinner out a week to, say, marriage. (At this point, we feel obliged to remind you that when it comes to hijackers and terrorists, the greater and more urgent their demands become, the more evident it is to the authorities that they're completely crackers. If you catch our drift.) You've got a bee in your bonnet, and it's buzzing commitment. You're obsessed with pinning him down; it's the fulcrum on which your entire life balances. Danger, danger: Any situation that requires the use of the phrase "your entire life" can often mean big trouble.

Such a fate befell Vicki, a twenty-five-year-old book editor in New York, and her boyfriend Tim. They'd been going out for three and a half years when they decided to move in together.

"Tim's lease was up and it seemed like a good idea. For some reason, though, I didn't want to live together until we were engaged. I don't know why I felt that way; now it seems unnecessary. But I was insecure in the relationship—I was always jealous, asking him a million questions, wanting to know what he did every second of the day. I was convinced that marriage would make me feel more secure. It seemed to me that we had been going out for so long, the next logical thing for us to do was get engaged and then live together. In that order. And I let him know it, again and again.

"He finally proposed when we were on a vacation in Hawaii. Now I realize that being engaged didn't mean the same thing to him that it did to me. For me, it was the first step toward the ultimate goal. For him, it was just a ticket to living with me in my apartment. He moved in and everything was fine.

"But then I wanted more. I needed to plan the wedding. My brain was practically chanting, 'Set a date, set a date.' It didn't help that my mother was calling every day, nagging me to reserve a wedding location. Tim had wanted to keep the whole thing really low-key; he didn't want to tell people right away. He kept assuring me that we would one day get married, but he didn't want to make a big deal of the engagement. I did. 'One day' wasn't specific enough for me. I persisted, and finally he relented. We reserved a night at our country club. And I was happy.

"He wasn't, though. He wouldn't help me register or look at furniture. He hated everything I picked. He couldn't seem to get around to picking ushers. I had always had this picture in my head of what an engagement was supposed to be — and he wasn't delivering. I kept at him to participate in my plans. He grew more and more disagreeable. I asked him a thousand times a day what was wrong; he kept insisting that everything was fine.

"Obviously, it wasn't. Things started falling apart. We began to make social plans with other people — it was too depressing to be alone together. One weekend, three months before the wedding, I went to visit friends in the Hamptons. When I got back, he told me how much he had missed me. Instead of telling him I'd missed him too, I demanded to know what he had done all weekend, who he'd seen, who he'd talked to. The same old stuff. He started crying and told me that he just couldn't go on this way. He said he needed to be able to make his own decisions, live his own life. He moved out."

. . .

You can lead a boy to the altar, but you can't make him say, "I do." For Vicki, that was a tough lesson to learn. And while she thirsted for marriage, Mary, thirty-three, would have settled for monogamy. She met Rob when she was working as a producer for a local New York television talk show. He was an expert guest. He was cute, witty, and had a big . . . intellect. She thought they were perfect for each other. She couldn't have been more wrong.

"I didn't know he was seeing someone else until I had already slept with him. He told me that he and Peggy had been together three years—and my heart fell to my knees—but then he said it was almost over. Of course I believed him. He asked if I wanted him to break it off immediately with her for me, and I said no. My first mistake.

"A month later, he still hadn't ended it. He also hadn't invited me out to meet his friends or his family, although he kept promising he would. We had a bedroom relationship— not that it was all sex, but that's just where we spent all our time. I stayed with it because I was still impressed by his credentials, his grasp (literally and figuratively) of the issues, his experience.

"Two months went by, and I assumed that he had finally ended it with Peggy. I asked him how it went, how did she take it. He said he hadn't broken it off yet. I was shocked. I started feeling like the other woman. I didn't like the feeling of being taken advantage of. Our relationship became half passion, half disillusionment. It was so strange, not a normal boyfriend-girlfriend thing, more like some amorphic beast. Still, I was crazy in love with him.

"I focused all my anger on this phantom Peggy. I fixated on her even though I had never met her. She was always there with us, in bed, in my mind. All our problems were about her and his inability to break up with her. I threw tantrums. I cried.

I complained. All about her. This made it easier to refuse to commit to me—who wants to pledge devotion to psycho-woman? I grilled him for information about her. I said things like, 'Why don't you want me? I'm young and exciting. What's she got that I don't have?" He wouldn't say anything, and that made me angrier. I pressured him constantly. Eventually, it felt like I was just pressuring him to hurt me."

Love is not a democracy. No matter how hard you campaign, you can't make him love you, marry you, or commit to you if he doesn't want to. "Basically," says Dr. Sills, "if you want to move forward but your partner wants to stay in the same place, you've got an irreconcilable conflict of interest. Someone's got to give in—or it ends." Your best bet, she says, is to back off for as long as you can and see how the situation develops. But eventually, if he can't meet your needs, you'll have to find someone who can. In short:

COMMITMENT LUST

How it works: You demand marriage, monogamy, regular sex, you name it, from a man who cannot, by nature, take orders from anyone and like it. He reacts by . . . not reacting. **How it makes you feel:** Like you're beating your head against a brick wall. Your words and sentences start to sound the same. In fact, they are the same. You've become a single-track person in a multitrack world. You're even boring yourself. **Overriding emotion:** Frustration. No one seems to understand how important this is! Why doesn't anyone see how important this is? This is important! **How you should react:** Back off. Remember when the neighborhood kids tried to feed you dirt and you said, "You can't make me." The same goes for him. **How you do react:** You insist on trying to feed him dirt, ten, twenty times a day. Why won't he eat dirt? Will he ever eat dirt? If so, when? **The upside:** You learn the difference between "Will you, please?" and "Do it—or else." You opt for the former. This makes you a more pleasant person. The kind of person that people want to do things for. The kind of person that someone might want to be with . . . for his entire life, even. It's worth considering.

5. A Current Affair (or, Cheaters Never Prosper)

Oy, such a chapter we've had—a regular Pandora's box of trials and fibrillations. So far, we've seen him refuse to a) give you the love you need, b) modify his behavior, c) say one nice thing to you, and d) make a commitment. But wait, there's more. The last bomb on the heartbreak minefield has yet to explode. Brace yourself—many consider it to be the most combustible of them all. The Big Dread One. Its hideous name: infidelity.

Now before we continue, let's banish any sexist stereotypes. Men aren't the only ones who stray; low-fidelity is an equal-opportunity vice. In some cases, yes, it's the man who is lying, cheating, and sliming his filthy alley-cat way all over town. In other cases, however, it's the woman who's having a quiet, tasteful, and totally justifiable little indiscretion. We just wanted to make that clear.

Ursula, twenty-five, and Peter were a textbook infidelity case. After three years, the relationship had become rocky; he had already begun to distance her (remember that old trick?) in various ways. But the straw that broke the relationship's back was yet to come.

"I was living in Boston, taking graduate classes at Harvard," Ursula says. "I had moved there after college to be with Peter. I had just finished my midterm exams. I had one free weekend between semesters, and I assumed that Peter and I would spend it together. Instead, he told me that he had made plans to visit his friend Sam in Philadelphia. I protested; I thought it was strange because he had been visiting Sam a lot.

"When he came back home after that weekend, he called me up and told me that the real reason he went to Philly was to take a girl from the University of Pennsylvania to some dance. He had seen her several times before, on previous weekends. He said he slept with her but they didn't have sex. Right. It didn't matter anyway; it wasn't the sex, it was the deceit. I felt like a fool. I was so hurt. I said, that's it, I'm not dealing with this. He drove me to it, though. And although he didn't sound really happy that I was ending it, he didn't object vociferously, either."

If you've never cheated or been cheated on, it's possible that you'll read this story and think, what's the big deal? How can a few misplaced push-ups diffuse the power of true love? This Peter guy didn't even have sex with that girl—what's Ursula's problem?

If you have, however, had a brush with cuckolding—or maybe you just have a friend who has—you can empathize with Ursula completely. Because you know that cheating isn't just about sex, it's about deception and cunning and calculation. It's about betrayal. And that's the kind of stuff that can bring a relationship to its figurative knees.

Which is not to say that a relationship can never survive such a problem. In particular, one-night stands can often be forgiven (but not forgotten, dammit) because they're isolated affairs as opposed to extended indiscretions. In the case of the one-night stand, both parties can often come to an understanding because they recognize that maybe THAT NIGHT was a cry for help or a symptom of fear and confusion. They agree to overlook THAT NIGHT because it occurred due to extenuating circumstances such as blind rage or extreme intoxication.

Or maybe, just maybe, THAT NIGHT isn't discussed at all because the perpetrator *never got caught.*

Oooooh, we have chills. We're going to disregard that last possibility. We're also going to acknowledge the fact that people do not have a fixed capacity for feeling: Just because someone is with a second person doesn't mean he or she loves the first person any less. It does mean, however, that he or she loves the first person in a different way. And it also implies that the unfaithful one is looking for something that he or she isn't getting from the relationship. That the relationship isn't a satisfactory or happy or productive one. And that there's a good chance that said relationship will end.

Dr. Sills believes that people are unfaithful for four reasons: lust (the temptation was beyond his resistance—would you kick Cindy Crawford out of bed?), ego/insecurity (he'd been feeling so ugly lately), a need for freedom (he felt trapped, tense—that trip around the world didn't quite take the pressure off), and anger (you called him an idiot in front of his boss; what else did you expect?). Often, the reasons can mix and match. For example . . .

VAL: The very, very, very few times I've been led astray, I did it as revenge—I was angry that I was putting more into the relationship than I was getting back. I would sleep with someone else and then tell my boyfriend right afterwards, to hurt him. But my own insecurity factored into these liaisons, also. I felt ignored by the boyfriend, so I would sleep with the other guy to get attention—from both of them.

ELLEN: But if you were angry and insecure in the relationship, why didn't you just end it?

V: I don't know. I guess I liked my boyfriend better.

E: I know what you mean. Hey, I loved my boyfriend and I still cheated on him.

v: (sanctimoniously): Well, you know, if you're conscious that your actions can hurt someone, maybe you don't really love them after all . . .

E: (mockingly): Thus saith the preacher. In my case, though, I would have to say that I dabbled on the side to prove to myself that I wasn't trapped in the relationship—so I wouldn't have to grow up. I did it for the freedom.

v: But what about all those times you said you were looking for some passion, some excitement?

E: Okay. So I did it for the lust. No, the freedom. No, the lust. No, the freedom. No, the . . .

v: Okay, okay, all of the above. Didn't you feel guilty, though?

E: The funny thing is, I didn't. I told my boyfriends that I wanted to date other people and they said okay. So I would say to myself, 'I'm not married. I'm entitled.'

v: Really? I practically threw myself on the floor and begged for forgiveness.

E: Well, I did throw myself on the floor . . .

v: I bet you did.

Our point is that the cause of infidelity is more often than not a psychological smorgasbord. Not that this makes the dirty deed any less reprehensible. But can anyone really throw the first stone? Think about it. Many people who claim they would never two-time probably have, in some way or another. One person we know never actually slept with two women at the same time, but he spent several consecutive relationships obsessed with—psychologically committed—to another, unobtainable woman. He couldn't be with the one he loved, so he loved the one he was with. That's not being completely faithful, is it? Or look at Ellen, who insists that she never technically cheated, because her boyfriends agreed to nonexclusivity. Technicalities are irrelevant; they don't change the fact that her relationships were defective—and didn't prevent them from eventually coming to an end. To conclude:

A CURRENT AFFAIR

How it works: It's pretty self-explanatory, really. If you don't know, you're better off not knowing. **How it makes you feel:** If you're the one being cheated on, your self-esteem plummets. You feel betrayed, duped, and angry. Usually it's enough to make you hightail it the hell out of the relationship. If you're the one doing the cheating, you feel furtive, invigorated, guilty. At first you might feel like you've got everything in control; you know what you're doing and no one will get hurt. But if the affair continues, your mind starts to reel. You feel as though you're careening down a hill in a car with no brakes. You don't know what will happen next. **Overriding emotions:** Either way, you eventually feel rock-bottom low. Infidelity creates an all-time emotional nadir. Your current relationship doesn't make you happy. If you're having an affair, in time that won't make you happy, either. You wonder what you're looking for. You wonder if you'll ever find it. **How you should react:** If you're being cheated on, get out now. If you're cheating, figure out how important your current relationship is to you, and govern yourself accordingly. Face it, sweetie: You can't have your cake and eat it too. **How you do react:** Surprisingly, you react the way you should react. There's nothing else you can do, really. **The upside:** You're faced with the ultimate character test. You're forced to assess your relationship immediately and make a decision. For once, you can't procrastinate. You come out of it a sadder but wiser person. No kidding. Which brings us to the end of The Beginning of the End. What have you learned? We know we learned a lot just from putting all this down. But our educational experience isn't really the issue right now. So, in our never-ending quest to improve your reading comprehension and make your life better, we've created a little multiple-choice pop quiz. There are no right or wrong answers. Which, in the world of heartbreak, is exactly as it should be.

Beginning-of-the-End Quiz

Question 1: He's been acting weird. You're not sure, but you're afraid that trouble's afoot. Does he:

a. insist that he loves you and needs you—but he'll miss you, since he's going away for the fifth weekend in a row to "bond with his brother"?
b. refuse to kiss you with his whole mouth, even after you've brushed your teeth?
c. sigh wistfully when he sees a beer commercial?
d. tell you he doesn't mind if you go kayaking on the Colorado River without a life jacket—or a kayak?
e. hold you tight, rock you gently, and cry while insisting that you deserve better?

Answer: If you circled any of the above—be afraid. Be very afraid.

Question 2: Could this mean the love is fading? You can't believe it. And yet, do you still find yourself:

a. inquiring a mite too often about the new receptionist with the big hair at his office?
b. having lunch with said receptionist and grilling her for information?
c. holding his unopened mail up to the light and/or the steam of a whistling teakettle?
d. hunting like a woman possessed through his drawers for

you-don't-know-what-but-you'll-recognize-it-when-you-
see-it?

e. picking up the messages on his machine (of course you
know his code, you canny girl) and then going insane
because that woman "Cecile" keeps calling him about his
"overdue MasterCard bill"?

Answer: If you circled any of the above, your paranoia is showing. And while a healthy dose of jealousy is normal, moonlighting
as a detective is something else entirely. Little tip: If you don't trust
him, it's not a good sign.

Question 3: You're listening to the radio and a sad song about
waning romance comes on. Do you:

a. change stations?
b. weep uncontrollably and claw at the furniture?
c. mournfully howl, "It's true, it's all true"?
d. suddenly proclaim the songwriter a genius, even though
his videos consist primarily of blonde, scantily clad, tat-
tooed girls chained to motorcycles?
e. whip out your .38 special and blow your stereo receiver to
kingdom come?

Answer: If you circled a through d, you're either on an intense
hormonal jag, have flashed back to a pathetic former life, or are,
indeed, at the beginning of the end. If you circled e, we suggest
you seek professional help, pronto.

Question 4: In the beginning of the beginning, the two of you had
so much in common. Nowadays, you:

a. can't believe that you ever thought the smoked-glass-and-
lacquer furniture in his apartment was anything but the
devil's handiwork. You feel compelled to tell him this,
often.

b. have severely unbalanced libidos—and shattered egos, to match.

c. notice that even though neither of you ever was much for working out, recently he's been doing an awful lot of it by himself. Not to be outdone, you lift and hurl insults, epithets, and heavy, sodden tissues daily.

d. have acquired a sudden distaste for each other's friends and family.

e. share only rising resentment and frustration.

Answer: Although an occasional squabble is to be expected, if you circled any of the above, you've passed the limits of healthy dissent. Especially if you circled e, fasten your seat belt—it's going to be a bumpy ride.

Question 5: You're having dinner with your friend/mother/sympathetic colleague. You suddenly burst into tears. When she asks you what's wrong, you say:

a. "I asked for salad dressing on the side."
b. "What do you mean? I always do this when I'm happy."
c. "Waiter, there's misery and destruction in my soup."
d. "Oh, nothing—just my entire life, that's all."
e. "I know I'll never love this way again."

Answer: If you circled a or b, you're in deep denial. If you circled c, try to lighten up a little; that thing in your soup may look like misery and destruction, but here on Earth, we call it a fly. If you circled d or e, you have a taste for melodrama, as well as salad dressing on the side. And by the way, if you circled any of the above, well, we hate to break it to you, but . . .

Question 6: . . . it's a distinct possibility: Your relationship is about to end. Will you:

a. claim victim status and make sure everyone feels sorry for you?
b. avoid the breakup and your unhappiness for as long as you can?
c. end it even though you don't really want to because you know how hard it is for him to hurt you?
d. demand an explanation and really make him sweat?
e. be the big person and behave with dignity even though you'd rather be small and petty and break things?

Answer: Read chapter 2.

2

The Final Curtain

SO IT'S come to this, has it? After weeks of preparation, you're facing the final curtain. One of you has uttered the six little words that are intrinsic to every breakup: We have to talk—it's over. You fuse together in the traditional vise-grip farewell hug. If you're in your apartment, you squelch the urge to barricade all exits. If you're in his apartment, you refrain from nailing yourself to the door frame. And in the frozen millisecond after you've said good-bye, in that first horrible instant of boyfriendless-ness, you realize that you've never loved him more than you do at this precise moment.

Welcome to the Heartbreak Express. Sorry to have you aboard. Odds are, even if you were forewarned and forearmed, you're feeling a little dazed—how did you get here, when did you buy your ticket, who booked you with such a ridiculously high, nonrefundable fare? Well, as someone once said (we think it was Huey Lewis, but maybe it was Hercule Poirot), you don't need no credit card to ride this train. Fortunately, there is such thing as a free ride. Unfortunately, it's to hell and back.

But before you look at the instruction card in the seat pocket in front of you, let's talk about the preliminary boarding procedures. There are many ways to jump on the breakup bandwagon, because there are many different kinds of breakups. Some are mutual and amicable, some are sudden and jarring, others are actually civil — wars, that is. Some happen in person; others utilize less personal means, like letters, or higher-tech methods, like phones, faxes, and even telegrams (no joke — we heard of one arbitrage trader who telegraphed the bad news to his fiancée from Japan as follows: "No yen for you — stop. Am not coming back to New York — stop. If you're thinking of chasing after me — stop. It's time for this relationship to — stop." Jeez. No word-waster, he).

There are many ways to say good-bye to love. And while they all generally have the same end result (namely, misery) their various incarnations can elicit different degrees of emotion. Here, the most universal types of the common household breakup — and how they make you feel.

1. The Fake-outs

We're gonna start you off easy. In a world of false starts, it seems only fitting that there be false ends, too. Hence, the Break Up To Make Up category. Often, these situations are orchestrated to create high drama and rip-roaring post-breakup sex.

Diane, a twenty-six-year-old fashion industry forecaster, remembers how she and her boyfriend — now husband — "broke up and got back together at least once a week. It was the way we'd fight. Somehow, we couldn't get enough adrenaline flowing by exchanging the normal insults. We needed that hit of 'Oh my god, this could be the end' to shake us back to our senses. We had to be faced with the threat of not having each other in order to work hard at being together. Plus, the making-up part was totally exhilarating. It was a life of incredible peaks and valleys. I know it sounds sick, but for whatever reason, it worked for us. And now that we're married, we don't fight nearly as much. Maybe we were insecure about the relationship before we cemented it."

In other cases, however, fake breakups are merely dress rehearsals for the real thing. Couples break up and are too depressed to stay apart; they get back together, realize they're still depressed, and then break up again—this time for good.

When Leslie, twenty-six, and Jason broke up for the first time, "It was a real scene," she says. "We screamed and shouted and cried—it was like a scene out of a movie. The next day, when the adrenaline rush wore off, I felt stunned. Like we had done something rash. I don't know why—things had been miserable for about six months already; we both knew it was coming. But it all seemed so sudden. I moved around in a fog for a couple of days—and then he called. We talked for about an hour; after all, we had been going out for two years, and we missed each other. We made a plan to see each other, 'just to have dinner.' Not quite. We ended up sleeping together, and then we picked up like nothing had ever happened. For a while, things were better. But slowly, the same old problems began to crop up. Two months later, we broke up again, quietly, somberly—and for good."

Leslie and Jason's first breakup simply served as a step toward a more permanent termination. This is the most common function of fake breakups. Every now and then, though, when the planets are aligned just so, fake breakups become vehicles for change—they end up jump-starting a new, better relationship. Case in point: Callie and Bill.

"When I saw him after the breakup, months later," she says, "he was a whole different person. He was really committed to us. He said, 'I know I can't take back all the terrible things I've done, but I want to make things different with us. I love you. I want to make it work.' I agreed—reluctantly—and he was true to his word. It was like an entirely new relationship, a great one. We got married a year later."

Yes, Virginia, there is such thing as a happy ending. How do you know if your breakup is the genuine article? Take this quiz and find out.

PART ONE: THE WAY YOU SEE IT
True or False?

1. You have had enough, dagnabbit.
2. When you look at him, you see a selfish jerk who doesn't give a hoot about your needs.
3. If you never saw him again, it would be too soon.
4. Whenever you think about (horrible) him, you burst into tears.
5. You wish you had a plate or an anvil or something handy to hurl at his bulbous head.
6. You tried so hard to care about his aching back, but you just couldn't.
7. When he talked about stuff like your relationship and where it was headed, you zoned out and thought about what you were going to wear to work the next day.
8. When he made overtures in bed, you went along, even if you weren't particularly in the mood, because it was easier to do it than to say no.
9. When you look at him, you see an average Joe.

10. If you never saw him again, it would be too bad, but you'd get past it.

If you answered true to questions one through five, try to lighten up. It can't be more than, what, a week since you and your guy moved to Splitsville? You're obviously feeling a little volatile. That's fine. Your womanly emotions are as powerful as the tides — let them flow — and they're not necessarily running a perfectly straight course. Today, you may never want to lay eyes on him again, but tomorrow could be a different story. Any kind of powerful feeling — love, hate, a Dove Bar craving — cannot be denied. Much as you may be loath to admit it, you still care about the selfish jerk. So don't write him off entirely. Yet.

If you answered true to questions six through ten, you don't seem to care anymore. And, although you're undoubtedly sad to see the relationship end, you probably know in your heart of hearts that it's for the best. As someone once said (we think it was Stevie Nicks, but maybe it was Coco Chanel), you can never break the chain. In other words, if you don't love him now, you may never love him again. Cut your losses and move on.

PART TWO: INTERPRETING THE WAY HE SEES IT
True or False?

1. He got a hard-on when you hugged good-bye forever.
2. "Fine," he said. "If this is what you want."
3. He looked like shit at the last dinner.
4. In the flurry of emotions, he failed to ask you to send him his Springsteen CDs.
5. He bumped into the waiter when he stormed off.
6. He offered to get you a cab after the breakup.

7. Even in the flurry of emotion, he still managed to remind you to send him his contact lens solution.
8. "I'm not a teenager anymore," he responded when you queried as to why you hadn't had sex in the last month.
9. He brought flowers to the last dinner.
10. He said that he hates you, it's over, and he never wants to see you again. OR, he said that he's sorry, he tried, but he doesn't love you anymore.

If you answered true to questions one through five, there's probably hope if you want it. He's angry and defensive— positions you're familiar with, we're sure. He's probably confused, too, which he must hate since it means that he isn't in *complete control.* God forbid. What to watch for in the days to come: If he acts like nothing ever happened, then he doesn't want it to be over. He'll treat you like you never broke up. Since he still feels that he loves you, why shouldn't he act that way?

If you answered true to questions six through ten, kiss this relationship *sayonara.* Guys are easier to interpret than we complex female beings. When we say something, we sometimes mean the opposite—and sometimes we don't— and we expect everyone else to be able to read our minds. Men say what they mean, especially when they're talking about hunger and thirst levels—or love. Sure, there are exceptions, but by and large, men are too straightforward to attempt hidden meaning. If he says he doesn't love you, he doesn't. If he brought flowers to dinner or offers to get you a cab, he is feeling guilty but unwavering in his attempt to leave you. If he has the presence of mind to ask for his stuff, he's not that shattered. So pick up the pieces of *your* shattered life and move on.

PART THREE: THE LAST QUESTION

Yes or No?

When you looked each other in the eyes after saying farewell, did you see even the slightest glimmer of love left? No cheating here.

If you answered yes, put down this book (keeping it, of course, for future reference) and throw yourself wholeheartedly into making the love work.

If you answered no, read on.

2. The Force-outs

So here we are, hitting the hard stuff—real breakups, we mean. This is the classic passive-aggressive maneuver: One member of a relationship wants to sever ties but refuses to say so. Finally, things get so bad that the other member is forced to do the dirty deed. This is tantamount to a boss not wanting to fire an employee, but making life in the office so miserable for that employee that he or she finally up and quits. Such was the case for Val and Mark, who ended things—

VAL: Martyr style. As is fitting with my Jewish heritage.

ELLEN: Mark was Jewish too, wasn't he?

V: Still is. He's not dead, you know.

E: He is to us.

V: (after a moment of funereal silence): Anyway. The end wasn't as bloody as the beginning of the end. Our levels of intimacy had steadily waned for about a month, but we were still talking at least once a day. Then, a day went by and he didn't call. And then another day. I wasn't going to call him . . .

E: . . . God forbid . . .

V: . . . so I waited. Four whole days, I waited. I went to my parents' house in New Jersey for the weekend so I wouldn't be sitting by the phone. Of course I called in for messages every ten minutes, anyway. My mom took me to see *Pretty Woman* to cheer me up. I cried. Sobbed. Huge gasps for air, lung-racking inhales—I was practically keening. Mom had to take me home before Julia Roberts even told Richard Gere that . . .

E: Yeah, yeah, yeah. Then what happened?

V: So then, on Monday, I came back to the city. My roommate told me there had been no calls—as if I didn't know that already. I couldn't wait any longer, so I had my friend Nancy call Mark and say she was looking for me. She pretended that she was worried about me, that she thought I had been in a terrible accident or something.

E: Of course he saw right through this.

V: And he still didn't call! Finally, I called Tuesday night and said "Look, Mark, do you want to break up with me?" He said, "I feel like we should just be friends."

E: Meaning he still liked you as a person but didn't want to stick it in anymore.

V: Harsh, but true. So I said, "Why didn't you call and tell me how you felt?" He said, "I didn't want to hurt you." I said, "So then don't break up with me." Apparently, that wasn't an option. So I ended up doing his dirty work for him—he told his friends that I broke up with him, and he came out of the whole thing smelling like a big, fat, lying, stinking, no-good rose!

E: (sensing that Val might be getting a bit overwrought): Val, calm down. It's been three years already.

V (rocking and holding her stomach): It still hurts, it still hurts.

E: What, the Death of Mark?

V: Yeah.

The unfortunate fact that Mark was too much of a pantywaist to tell Val the truth accomplished two things: 1) Mark was revealed as a wimp who wasn't worthy of Val's love, and 2) Val was denied a quick emotional recovery, because she couldn't let herself get angry at him. She kept rationalizing that he really loved her so much that he was trying to protect her, even while Ellen was trying to explain to her that he was a wimp who wasn't worthy of her love. Eventually, however, Val was able to realize that Mark's silence was indeed hurtful, got mad (more on that later), got even (she's writing a book about it, after all)—and then, finally, got over it.

3. The Get-Out-and-Stay-Outs!

These breakups are decisive and showy—with each party energetically doing his or her own dirty work, thanks very much. They're the four-alarm breakups, the kind that you see in the movies and want to avoid at all costs in real life. They are usually enacted by big movie fans. And they often entail a lot of screaming and howling and, with any luck, a dramatic splash of blood. That's what happened to Andrea, twenty-four, who started a small ad agency with Don, her boyfriend of four years. The breakup went something like this:

THE SCENE
Don and Andrea are walking together silently down a street in New York. It is a beautiful, sunny Friday afternoon. Don breaks the silence.

DON: We need to talk. I think it would be a good idea if you didn't come into the office anymore.
ANDREA: What do you mean?
DON (woodenly): I think you undermine my authority. No one

in the place argues with me except for you. It's not working. We can't get along. I don't think you should come in anymore.

ANDREA (shocked): Are you firing me?

DON (hedging): No. I mean, well, no. You can still do work—from home. I just can't have you in the office, because you don't treat me like an authority figure.

ANDREA (incensed): You're firing me! Just say it. Just look me in the eye and say, "Andrea, you're fired."

DON (defensively): No. I won't say that. Besides, we've put our relationship on the back burner for so long so that we could work on starting this company; now we can get office problems out of the way and work on our relationship.

ANDREA (acidly): Excuse me? What relationship? Our relationship is nonexistent. The only thing I have any feeling for is the agency.

DON (With infuriatingly brisk efficiency): I'm sorry to hear that. At any rate, we're prepared to pay you [a measly amount of] money for your stock holdings in the company. And, of course, we'll give you a couple of weeks of your [equally measly] salary to live on for a little while. I know everyone in the office will miss you very much.

ANDREA (suspiciously): What do you mean you know everyone in the office will miss me? Do you mean to tell me that you told everyone about this before you told me?

DON (counting off on his fingers): Well, I mean, not everyone. I told my father, of course. And my cousin, Randy. And a few of the people in the office, like my friend Bob. I talked to Bob about taking your place, actually. And then, naturally, I had to tell the art director and his assistant, and then your assistant . . .

Don's speech is interrupted by a fist flying into his face. Andrea's fist. There is a squishy, slamming noise, then blood flies in a graceful arc and splatters on the sidewalk. Andrea notices how it glistens in the sun. Don has never been punched before, so he looks a little shocked and panicky. He sits down on the curb, clutches his nose, and starts to cry. It's a messy moment.

DON (in gasps): Whadja . . . hafta . . . do that . . . for?

ANDREA (strangely calm): Well, I must say I'm relieved. I was beginning to think you were bloodless. Hm. I guess this means it's over.

Quite a little scene. And while we don't recommend that you try this at home, for Andrea it provided a certain satisfaction. "I realized," she now says, "that punching him was the only way that I could ever get to him, that I could ever make him *feel*. I'm not a violent person at all; I had never hit anyone before in my life. But he was so self-centered, so insensitive. He never would have been able to admit to himself that he had done anything wrong. It was pretty much the only way I could communicate the fact that I thought he had been unfair, unethical. Afterward, I felt no regrets. I just felt fortunate that I had landed such a lucky punch. And I never missed him or felt sad about the end of our relationship. In that one moment of insanity, I found closure." The only thing that rankles her about the whole affair, she adds, is that he still owes her some money. Which just goes to show you that, although violence is almost never a solution, in certain instances a little chutzpah can go a long way toward attaining peace of mind.

4. The Freak-outs

This is when things unravel so fast, you wonder: Did we really break up, or did I just dream it? Helen and Bob are one such example.

· · ·

"I was shocked the day of the breakup," says Helen, thirty. "We had been together for two years—although we had broken up and gotten back together a couple times. Come to think of it, every time we called it off, he'd say, 'If we were married, we'd work it out, but since we're not, let's break up.' What a jerk.

"The final breakup happened just after he'd gotten a new job at a corporate law firm," she says. "He was all high on becoming a corporate drone, so we went to Barneys, this fancy department store, to buy him some new suits. I spent the whole day helping him pick stuff out, acting like a good wife, pretending I wasn't bored. When we walked out of the store, he turned to me and said, 'This isn't working out. I can't do it anymore. Good-bye.' I was so stunned, I said, 'Okay. I'll see you around,' and walked away. I was in such a daze, I didn't know where I was. My knees were shaking; I broke out in a sweat. I wandered around for a while in a fog and eventually ended up in Union Square Park. I sort of came to when I suddenly found myself surrounded by a Puerto Rican soccer team—all eleven players. They must have just won a game and they were excited, whooping and jostling and hassling me. It was even more surreal because they were all speaking Spanish. I finally walked all the way home to the Upper East Side—three miles—and collapsed in my apartment. I had physical cramps. It was torture."

Jessica, twenty-five, experienced similar shock and confusion when she and Evan called it quits.

"Things had been bad. He was unsupportive, I was unhappy. We kept saying we were going to end it, but it dragged on. Finally, I went to upstate New York, ostensibly to visit friends but really in hopes of seeing him. I went with my friends to this one bar where everyone goes, and I stared at the door all night, but he never showed. Finally, as we were leaving, he pulled into the parking lot. He saw me and smiled and said, 'Get in.' He looked great; my control crumpled and I got in the car. As if on cue, our song came on the radio. We went back to his apartment. He cried and said he didn't know what he wanted. That he thought he wanted to marry me, but he also wanted to do his own thing for a while. Although he was indecisive, he was also really warm and loving.

"The next night," she says, "we were at the same bar, and after a few beers, he asked me, 'Would it be wrong if I invited you back to my place?' I went. We got to his apartment and had great sex. He was still inside me, and I looked up at him and thought about how happy I was. He looked down at me and said, 'God, I'm going to miss you.' What I thought was a welcome-back reunion, he just saw as a good-bye fuck. He drove me back to where I was staying—he didn't want me to spend the night—and that was the end of that."

It's no picnic to get blindsided that way. To make matters worse, Evan continued to call Jessica for months after their little exchange of words and fluids. "What kills me the most is that I allowed him to call and say he missed me and tell me that he was sorry it ended that way," Jessica now says. "I wish I hadn't. I knew it was over; the scars reopened every time I spoke to him. If there was one thing I learned from all this, it was that when you break up with someone, you should cut it off immediately. Don't let it drag on."

As always, hindsight is 20/20. But in the throes of a breakup, not everyone sees clearly, nor eye-to-eye, for that matter. It's hard to behave perfectly in those last few minutes before you part ways with *the greatest love of your life*. And frankly, we don't think you should be expected to. If you are a stickler for propriety, however, may we suggest . . .

5. The Best Way Out

Our prototype edition. The display-case breakup. The floor model. We're sad to say that this horribly mature and well-mannered but heartrending tale comes straight from the life of . . .

ELLEN: Well, color me lucky.

VAL: I know it's hard for emotionally stilted people like you to spill their life's tragedies, but give it a go.

E: Okay. One night, Jake just showed up at my apartment. Unannounced. At first, when the doorman buzzed him up, I was annoyed. I mean, what if I hadn't been alone? [Remember, dear reader, Ellen's little infidelity tic.] Anyway, when I answered the door, I said, "You know, you can't just show up here like this." He sighed and said, "I know. I'm sorry, El, I was just taking a walk, and I . . . I . . . thought I'd stop in." He looked so apologetic; he just stood there and dripped—it was pouring rain outside. I was mollified and said, "Never mind, it's okay," and went to hug and kiss him hello. He wrapped his arms around me and held me so tightly and lovingly, stroking my hair, that . . . that . . .

V: Take your time . . .

E: That I immediately knew something was wrong. I looked at his face, and it was so weary and lined. I said, "What's the matter?" He said—of course—"We need to talk." I said, "About what?" He said,

V: "About us."

E: Right. We sat on the edge of the bed, gingerly, like we weren't quite sure if it would support our weight. He kept hemming and hawing and clearing his throat, not able to articulate anything. He held his head in his hands, as if it suddenly weighed a hundred pounds. It was too painful for me to watch him try to choke out the words, so I finally leaned my head on his arm, shut my eyes, and asked, "Do you not want to go out anymore?" He answered, "I think I don't." So I said, "Okay."

v: That's it? "Okay"? Just like that?

E: That's exactly what he said. I asked him, "What else is there to say?" Then I said, "There's nothing else left for us to do. My only regret is that we never were able to talk until there was nothing left to say. But other than that, I wouldn't take back a minute of my time with you. I wouldn't change a thing." He looked ashen. I felt numb and remote; our voices sounded to me like they were coming from a thousand miles away.

v: What did he say?

E: He said . . . well, he said, "Elly, you know you'll always be a part of me, a part of my life. You'll always be family." We sat there and stared at the floor for a little while. Then I told him he should go. The whole thing only took about five minutes, but it seemed like five lifetimes. We mumbled something about how we would always love each other and kissed one last, sad kiss. I felt like I was at my own funeral. We said good-bye.

v (quietly sobbing): Oh, god, that's so sad.

E: Val, get a grip. This isn't a movie.

Completely inadvertently, Ellen and Jake managed to orchestrate a perfect breakup. They didn't drag it out, they didn't mar the moment with petty comments or hostilities. They were calm and friendly. They ended things on a good, adult note. And then they both committed suicide (just kidding).

So you thought your breakup was bad? Well, it probably was. But since misery loves company, here are some of the worst breakup stories that we've harvested from our crop:

- A woman writes a Dear John letter to her boyfriend. He sends her back a photograph of him and another woman having sex. She, in turn, sends him a photo of her and another guy in a similarly compromising position. He sends said photo to her mother.

- A guy wants to call it quits with his girlfriend but doesn't know how. One day, the two of them are having a normal conversation, and she asks him, "What did you do today?" He answers, "I screwed your best friend." (And he had.) She promptly leaves him; he wins our prize as the Last of the Great Offenders.

- A man is in a car accident and has to stay in the hospital for a few weeks. His girlfriend stays by his side the entire time, attending to his every need. On the day of his release, he says, "You've been so nice, but I'm afraid that I've come to associate you with the accident, and I can't bear to look at you anymore."

- Three months before the wedding, a woman's fiancé walks into a glass door and suffers terrible head injuries. He is forced to undergo extensive physical therapy. He emerges from the experience a new man. A new man who has reconsidered the idea of marriage. A new man who now wants to try life as a swinging, sleazing bachelor. Needless to say, the nuptials are called off.

Wow. We feel better already. Maybe you do, too. Take a breather—you deserve it. But don't get too comfortable. Now that you know how you landed on this runaway train, it's time to buckle up, tuck away all sharp objects and eyeglasses, put your head between your legs, and, as the old saying goes, kiss your ass good-bye. The breakup being safely accomplished, you're about to embark on the next stage: The Worst Twenty-four Hours of Your Life. Or, as we're fond of calling it, chapter 3.

the top ten things you think of saying when you want to break it off:

10.

The dog ate my love for you.

9.

It's not you, it's me. I'm not attracted to you.

8.

I have good news and bad news. The good news is, you're going to be getting that "alone time" you've been wanting so badly.

7.

It's against my principles to sleep with more than ten men at a time. Then again, the other guys in your office don't seem to mind.

6.

I just love kids, don't you?

5.

I'll tell you where the love went—out the window, with your stupid Gameboy.

4.

I feel so comfortable with you, I don't care if I gain another twenty-five pounds.

3.

Two words: Platonic love.

2.

I should really show you a picture of me before all the surgery.

1.

How much cash can you scrape together by noon?

what you really do say:

Nothing's wrong. Honestly. Nothing.

top ten things you think of saying when someone breaks up with you:

10.
Can I put you on hold for one second?
9.
What a relief! I've been meaning to say the exact same thing to you!
8.
What, and be a single mother?
7.
Now there's a coincidence—Marvin Michelson was here not five minutes ago!
6.
And you are . . . ?
5.
You'll regret this. Maybe not today, maybe not tomorrow. But soon and for the rest of your stinking life.
4.
Can I have some money?
3.
For future reference, using the word *horny* in bed makes women sick.
2.
I want you to know that your little tax secrets are safe with me.
1.
Fine. I never liked you anyway.

what you do say:

(Choose one)
I can't believe this is happening.
I knew this would happen.
Why is this happening to me?

3

The Worst Twenty-four Hours of Your Life

THAT'S IT. Over. *Finis.* The fireworks have ended. The good-byes have ended. *The love has ended.* But the horror, the horror has only just begun.

We're not going to soft-peddle this. Breaking up with someone is no garden party. It's not even a really bad, awkward office party. But there is the proverbial silver lining: All things, misery included, have their boundaries (hey, even office parties come to their uncomfortable ends, don't they?). And although there's a pain where there once was a heart, the truth is, we human beings are remarkably resilient creatures. We can weather just about any storm. As someone once said (we think it was Shakespeare, but maybe it was Henry Luce): Time heals all wounds.

It's just passing the time that can be a real killer. When it comes to breakups, you don't get the worst of it when it happens. The ending is merely a prelude to the hell that follows. The first twenty-four hours are probably the bleakest of the estimated forty-five hundred hours it takes to get over a heartbreak. They won't go down easy. But before you choke to death on your own self-pity, try to assess the situation with an iota of optimism: Things can't get much worse, so odds are they'll get better. If you can make it to sunrise without putting your head in the oven, there's at least a slight chance that you'll have a shot at happiness at some point during, if not this lifetime, at least the next. And you've just managed to shed about 160 unwanted pounds, without doing a single stomach crunch.

VAL: Or 175 pounds, in your case. Lucky for Jake, he only had to shed 110 pounds, no, 104, no, 99 . . .

ELLEN: And the numbers got lower as time wore on. I was on a real heartbreak diet for a while there. Remember my first twenty-four hours? When Jake left, I sat on the floor, stunned, for about an hour. Then I called you. You answered the phone and you said —

V: "What's the matter?"

E: Right. I said, "Jake and I just broke up." You said —

V: "I'll be right over."

E: And it was pouring rain. You couldn't get a cab — you kept calling from each subway station you stopped at, saying —

V: "Hang on, El — I'll be there soon."

E: God, that was awful. When you finally got to my house, you sat down on the floor next to me and just looked at me with big, sorry eyes. You were afraid to touch me. You were afraid if you hugged me, I'd burst into tears. But I never really cried at all. Instead, we smoked about a hundred cigarettes . . .

V: My lungs hurt just thinking about it.

E: . . . and we did leg lifts and push-ups to distract ourselves.

v: Correction. You did leg lifts and push-ups. I watched.

E (nostalgically): I was so firm then.

v: Still are. And then we did the feelings update every hour or so. You went from feeling numb to low to malignant, back up to low. And then you had to go and play, "Brown Eyed Girl" . . .

E: It was Jake's and my song.

v: . . . and you hit rock bottom.

E: At which point I started writing.

v: Yeah, you wrote reams of poetry and never-to-be-sent letters to the old boy. Some pretty good ones.

E: Not really. I reread one just the other day and boy, was it maudlin. It's so hard to write good self-pitying verse; no one I know can do it. With one exception.

v: You flatter me.

E: So then you spent the night. The next morning—the worst day of my life—we went to work. I thought it was better to go and do something than sit around and analyze the horrible things I was feeling.

v: I had done most of that the night before, anyway.

E: At work, I acted as happy as I possibly could. As if I'd just won the lottery. I saw no reason for anyone to know that Jake and I had called it quits. We worked with a bunch of gossiping women—

v: There was no reason to let those bloodsuckers thrive on your misery.

E: Precisely. It was nobody's business but my own. And yours, of course.

v (nodding sagely): So this was an emotionally self-protective time.

E: More or less. That night, I watched TV with Howie, my best male friend. He brought me dinner, but I couldn't swallow a thing. He held my hand. The physical—not sexual—

contact was good; he made me feel loved and safe. He sat there until I went to sleep. I think I slept okay the first night. The sleeplessness came later.

v: It's weird—I suffered from insomnia before Mark and I even broke up. I couldn't eat; I smoked like a fiend. I cried constantly. My roommate at the time thought I was going to have a nervous breakdown.

e: But you managed to hold yourself together?

v: Barely. My first twenty-four hours, I stayed in bed all day and watched soap operas and ate Doritos. I called my friend Judy to give her the feelings update every ten minutes. I called my friend Sue and asked her to repeat (and repeat) the story of this dinner party she gave when Mark and I were happy. I called my mother, and she told me it was all my fault. She can always be counted on for reassuring comments like that. If I had known you then, I would have called you. But I didn't. So I called all my ex-boyfriends and asked them to come over and sleep with me. No takers. It was a miserable day.

e: Sounds.

v: I cried. I moaned. I considered cutting my own hair to further my agony. In some place in my head, I was thinking what great material it all would be for some future use. I felt like I was really living in my pain.

e: Nothing like a life blow to remind you that you're alive.

v: Exactly. But I'm especially self-punishing, thanks to Mom, and looking back, I think I sort of liked feeling that bad. I liked the melodrama.

e: I'll never understand that.

v: So after I decided not to cut my own hair, I did about ten shots of tequila, passed out, and thus cut short my worst twenty-four hours by about ten. I woke up and felt even worse. I feel sort of queasy just remembering it.

e: Ugh. I wish I drank, so I could be really sympathetic.

v: But you are anyway, aren't you?
e: Of course.
v: And that is why we're friends. (Val gets weepy, and even
   Ellen allows herself a sentimental moment.)

But enough about us. (What do *you* think about us?) Everyone
has a different method to her madness. When Stacy, a twenty-
eight-year-old magazine editor, broke up a four-year relationship with Zack, she eschewed Val and Ellen's support-system
technique and went for total solitude.

"We broke up at night," she says. "He stayed over because
he lived three hours away; he wanted to have sex, but I said
no—I was pissed that he would even want to. When he left,
early the next morning, I got up. I was a woman with a
mission. I went through my room, took anything that even
remotely reminded me of him, and dumped it. I threw out all
my underwear, and then gathered together the comforter on
the bed, clothes he had given me, clothes he had liked, posters
off my wall, books we had talked about, photographs, everything, and left it in the basement of my apartment building. I
purged myself completely; I didn't want a single trace of his
life in mine. I made a huge sweep of the place. I wasn't
throwing things around, though; I folded everything very
neatly, stacked it, and discarded it. I was sick of being emotional over him. I was coolheaded. I had a cold efficiency. I was
very methodical.

"I went to work and felt just terrible. It was like giving birth
or something. It was some terrible ordeal that I knew I would
have to go through in order to be happy and free. That night,
I came home and put on a nightgown, got a bottle of Scotch,
and sat on the couch. I didn't want to see anybody; I was
starting a new life, and I needed solitude to gain strength and
resolve for it. I went to bed early; I was deeply tired. And the
next day, I went out and bought myself all new things."

· · ·

Nice work, if you can afford it. In contrast to Stacy's desire for isolation, Sarah, twenty-six, sought companionship. Unfortunately, it was that of her (newly) ex-boyfriend.

"We had broken up the day before," she says, "and although it was already a done deal, I still had some things I wanted to say. At my urging, he agreed to meet me at a bookstore right near his apartment. I was early; he was on time. When he got there, I was in the self-help section.

"We talked more about why we shouldn't be going out, and even though I found myself agreeing, I also felt that I was still uncontrollably attracted to him. I started touching him on the hand, on the arm, on the back. He'd stiffen up and I noticed but didn't stop. We walked up and down the aisles for a few minutes, and then he turned to me and said, 'Can you please stop touching me like that?' I played dumb—and deaf. I don't know why I was acting this way; I must have been temporarily insane. I told him I'd stop. And I did until we stepped outside. Then the floodgates burst open. Right there, on the sidewalk, I pinned him against a streetlight and started kissing his neck. He pushed me away with more force than was necessary and started marching briskly toward his apartment building. I chased after him, apologizing. Once we got to his doorway, I asked him if he wanted me to come up so I could show him how sorry I was. He looked me square in the eye and said, 'I don't think so.' I spent the rest of the evening eating chopped liver sandwiches and drinking black cherry soda at our favorite deli. They had to ask me to leave at closing time. It was totally embarrassing."

We'll say. And while this isn't an approach we suggest, we're the first ones to acknowledge the fact that some things are beyond earthly control. The fact is, there is just no single ideal way to muddle through the first day or two. But—call us irrepressible—we're going to suggest one, anyway. Remember: Nothing's carved in stone here. Just take it an hour at a time, starting with . . .

8:35 P.M. You lock the door behind him. You're stunned. You feel weird, as though you've suddenly, without warning, moved to a neighboring town: Everything looks the same—your furniture, your clothes, the post office on the corner—but everything's just a little off. Wander around your apartment, dazed. Sit on the floor and try to cry—wonder why no tears are coming out. Open the refrigerator door and close it. Splash cold water on your face. Sit down carefully on the couch and say to yourself, maybe I'm okay, I don't need to cry, I'm doing fine. Think about this for a minute, hurl yourself face down in some pillows, and howl.

8:50 P.M. Come up for air. You still feel lousy, but at least that huge knot in your stomach has loosened up a little. Continue to weep steadily and maybe moan aloud to yourself, things along the lines of, "I'm so sad, why is this happening, how can I live without him?" This is good. This is known as catharsis, a release of emotions. If you bottled it all up and didn't let go, there's a good chance that six months down the road, you'd be on your way to work and something would snap and before you knew it, you'd be gunning down a load of school-children from a highway overpass. Keep crying.

8:57 P.M. Continue crying. The jackhammer-shaking of your hands has subsided to a more manageable saplings-in-a-hurri-cane quiver. You think you can use them now. Walk gingerly to the kitchen and drink something to replenish your tear glands (try to go decaf—the last thing you need now is the caffeine jitters). Entertain the idea of pushing yourself to the outer pain limits, making yourself *really feel*, by doing something like standing outside in the freezing cold without a coat on, or walking barefoot over burning coals—or calling your mother. Pick up the phone.

8:58 P.M. Put it down. Hey, you're heartbroken, not insane. Contemplate spending the evening alone, sitting on the floor, taking whiffs of his special dandruff shampoo and listening to "your" song. Actually go into the bathroom to search for the shampoo, but forget what you're looking for mid-search. Confused, call your best friend and tell her to beam herself into your apartment, immediately. If she's not home, leave an hysterical message on her answering machine (save the details for a more dramatic, face-to-face performance). Then, change into the mangiest, most comfortable clothes you own. Think despondently that this is what you'll probably be wearing for the rest of your life, since there won't be anyone around to admire your cute clothing ensembles and insouciant sense of style ever again.

9:15 P.M. Switch on the television. Remember how HE used to channel cruise with the remote and get all teary-eyed about it. Turn the volume way up. Turn the volume way down. Wonder where the hell your friend is; if *she* had just broken up with *her* boyfriend—if she *had* a boyfriend—you'd be over there comforting her by now, you can be sure of that. Sigh over how hard it is to get good friends these days. When the phone rings, jump up wildly, peel yourself off the ceiling, and then try not to hurl yourself through your glass coffee table when you realize that it's not HIM on the other end of the line, begging your forgiveness, but only your friend. Tell her that you need some company and some vodka. Not necessarily in that order.

10 P.M. Your friend arrives (and she certainly took her sweet time). Sit on the couch with her and re-create your tale of woe. Realize that some of the finer points are becoming blurry. *You're already forgetting him!* Burst into tears afresh, and allow your friend to pat you on the back and dole out tissues. Let her tell you how great you are, how smart, how sexy, how much of an ass he is to let such a jewel slip through his fingers. Get defensive because she called him an ass. Down a shot. Down another. *Nostrovia.*

11:30 P.M. Run out of alcohol. Flip between Leno and Letterman and debate over which one is more grating. Talk about the girl in your office who looks exactly like Jay Leno. Actually laugh a couple of times until you remember that this is no time for laughing. Or maybe it is. Try to figure out if there's any way you can get a joint at this hour.

12:30 A.M. Settle for one of your friend's cigarettes. Feel decadent and a little dazed and headachy from the combination of smoke, alcohol—and abject misery. Walk your friend to the door, making her promise to return tomorrow. Stare, glazed, at that thing that seems to be moving on the ceiling for about an hour and then go to bed.

1:40 A.M. Lie in bed with a cold towel over your face—just because your life is ruined doesn't mean you have to look like a Cabbage Patch Doll. Position yourself in the middle of the bed, feel uncomfortable, and move over to your customary side. Put pillows in the place where HE'd normally be. Make sure that Mr. Fluffy Bunny and a big box of tissues are within arm's reach.

4:30 A.M. Dream about him; jerk wide awake. Check to see if the phone is on the hook (why hasn't HE called, maybe something happened to him), sit up, and flip on the light. Dial the first three digits of his phone number and then hang up. Repeat as necessary. In desperation, call your sister—hey, she has to get up in a couple of hours anyway. When she answers, cross and sleepy, explain your emergency situation. Let her pour on the sympathy and then digress into how "our inability to sustain a productive relationship is really all because of Mom, you know." Marvel over how, every time you and your sister talk, the subject always turns to your mother. Get bored, hang up, and doze fitfully.

7:30 A.M. Throw your alarm clock across the room. Wake up and for one second, forget that HE's not lying next to you. Then, suddenly remember in a flood the events of last night. Hit rock bottom. Try to keep in mind that this is the worst you'll feel all day—make that all life. Don't prolong it; get up and out of bed, right away.

7:45 A.M. Fiddle with the hot and cold water knobs in the shower. Have trouble getting it just right. Wonder aloud if you'll ever get a break. Flash to the scene in *The Big Chill* when Glenn Close sobbed uncontrollably on the shower floor. Re-enact it. Somewhere in the back of your mind, enjoy the terrible drama of it all. Say, you're pretty good at this—maybe you should be a big Hollywood movie actress and when you're making your acceptance speech at the Academy Awards won't he be sorry? Realize that you've now been in the shower for nearly 45 minutes and could pass for a California Raisin. Get out, wrap yourself in a big, soft towel, and think of his arms. Take a corner of "his arms" and wipe out a hole in the steamed-up mirror. Look hard at yourself, your pain, your devastation. Know that there's no way in hell you can drag yourself to work today. Rationalize that this is for the sake of your co-workers. Sit on the toilet (lid down) and contemplate whether your whole relationship was one big lie.

9:30 A.M. Slowly come out of your reverie, chilled and undecided. Call in sick. Tell your boss you have a stabbing pain in your gut — it's the god's honest truth. Get back in bed.

11:00 A.M. Funny, you don't remember falling asleep. After clearing the mid-morning nap asbestos from your brain, decide that you had better get out of the house. Call a friend who works far, far away from your office and ask her if she wants to have lunch, right now. Well then, how about in ten minutes? An hour? Fine. Get dressed and feel just the tiniest bit self-satisfied that, even in these apocalyptic times, you can still put a good outfit together.

1:00 P.M. Get slightly miffed that your friend didn't spring for lunch. Has she no sensitivity? Remind yourself that if *she* had a three-martini lunch, you probably wouldn't feel inclined to support her sloppy habit, either. Get over it and enjoy your pleasant buzz. Feel a false sense of security and decide to shop until you drop. Fall into the nearest Gap and try on everything. Twice. Bring an armful of clothing to the register. The total comes to a rather staggering $400. Sober up instantly and winnow your choices down to a more reasonable $60. You feel bad enough without the additional heartbreak of next month's Visa bill. Decide that maybe you should go home before you do any more financial damage.

·   ·   ·

3:30 P.M. Walk in and see the blinking light on your answering machine—it's HIM! No, it's your boss. Freak out. Realize that, even in all your other worldly angst, life in the very real world requires you to stay employed. Freak out again. Take deep breaths and call your boss back. Somehow manage to convince her that you were at the doctor. Vow that the next time your heart gets ground into a million grains of sand, you won't play hooky. Vow that there won't be a next time. Collapse on the bed, your Gap bags all around, and feel one hot tear trickle sideways out of your eye.

4:15 P.M. Admire Oprah's impressive collection of dominatrices and the men who love them. These people are incredibly odd—some of the guys can't get off unless they're whipped within an inch of their lives. Then again, at least they're having sex. Wonder if HE thought you were too controlling. Wonder if you weren't controlling enough. Wonder how you'd look in a leather catsuit. Call a few of your friends and invite them to come over later tonight and bring you dinner.

6:15 P.M. Take two aspirin to ward off the small but certain hangover that's headed your way. Okay, you admit it, the martinis were a mistake. Try on your new clothes. Reject them. Your bedroom looks like the Salvation Army blew up—decide to clean the entire apartment before "Wheel of Fortune." Know in your heart of hearts that that would be unfeasible—do you try to do the impossible because you want to punish yourself when you inevitably fail? Consider getting back into therapy; settle instead for neatly hanging up your clothes. See HIS clothes in your closet. Get a giant garbage bag from the kitchen and put his things in it. His toothbrush. His stupid shampoo (oh yeah, *that's* what you were looking for). His boxer shorts. His pictures. Work up a sweat. Then put the bag out with the trash. Suddenly feel a surge of control—*you* should be a dominatrix on "Oprah." Giggle at the thought. Feel better for a second—but no longer than that.

7:30 P.M. One of your friends shows up, then another. They've brought you Chinese food. You had thought you wouldn't have much of an appetite, but those dumplings are looking mighty tempting. Polish them off. A third friend arrives. Apologize for eating all the dumplings. The four of you talk and talk about the previous night's events until it begins to seem like the whole horrible thing happened to someone else. You like that. Brag about how you bamboozled your boss, show off your new purchases, and in the middle of modeling The Classic White Shirt . . . burst into tears. Permit your friends to pet and pamper you until the squall passes. Then, sit quietly and hiccup for a little while, as they chat amongst themselves. Fortunately, you have great friends. Unfortunately, you don't have a boyfriend. Fortunately, neither do they. Unfortunately, who cares what they've got, *you've got nothing.*

11:00 P.M. Your last friend leaves. You lock the door behind her. You're stunned. You feel weird, as though you've suddenly, without warning, moved to a neighboring . . . oh, forget it. You're too tired to go through all this again. Besides which, you have to get some sleep—in the morning you're actually going to get up and function like a normal human being. You will go to work. You will not drink at lunch. You will not even think about blowing all your money on cheaply made, cleverly marketed clothing. So you made a few mistakes today—you're entitled. As someone once said (you think it was Scarlett O'Hara, but maybe it was Mr. Rogers), tomorrow is another day.

People say that music soothes the savage breast of heartache. We aren't so sure. But a little karaoke recuperation never hurt anyone. In fact, flexing those vocal cords with a few tunes might just make you feel, if not halfway decent, foolish enough to laugh at yourself. Give these old ditties a whirl:

Fooled Around and Fell in Love — Elvin Bishop

Funkytown — Lipps, Inc. (Just kidding — wanted to see if you were awake)

Go Your Own Way — Fleetwood Mac

Good Loving Gone Bad — Bad Company

Goodbye to Love — The Carpenters

How Blue Can You Get — B. B. King

How Can You Mend A Broken Heart? — Bee Gees

Hurting Each Other — The Carpenters

Hurts So Bad — Little Anthony and the Imperials

I Can Dream, Can't I? — Cole Porter

I Can't Make You Love Me — Bonnie Raitt

I Fall to Pieces — Patsy Cline

I Just Don't Know What to Do with Myself — Bob Dylan

I Know I'm Losing You — Rod Stewart

If You See Her — Bob Dylan

It's Too Late — Carole King

Just When I Needed You Most — Randy Vanwarmer

Keep On Loving You — REO Speedwagon

Kiss and Say Goodbye — Manhattans

Never Gonna Fall in Love Again — Eric Carmen

Not Enough Love in the World — Don Henley

Only Love Can Break Your Heart — Neil Young

Piece of My Heart — Janis Joplin

Please Mr., Please — Olivia Newton-John

Sara — Fleetwood Mac

Shannon — Henry Gross

Stop Dragging My Heart Around — Stevie Nicks and Tom Petty

Take the L Out of Lover and It's Over — Motels

Tears On My Pillow—Little Anthony and the Imperials
Total Eclipse of the Heart—Bonnie Tyler
We Just Disagree—Dave Mason
What'll I Do—Linda Ronstadt sings Irving Berlin
Who's Crying Now?—Journey
You've Lost That Loving Feeling—Righteous Brothers

Big bites of sorrow:

Derek and the Dominos' *Layla*
Fleetwood Mac's *Rumors*
Elton John's *Blue Moves*
Ricki Lee Jones' *Pirates*
John Lennon's *Walls and Bridges*
Joni Mitchell's *Blue*
Sinead O'Connor's *I Do Not Want What I Have Not Got*
Roy Orbison's *For the Lonely*
Frank Sinatra's *Songs for the Lonely*
The Smiths' *Queen Is Dead*
Bruce Springsteen's *Tunnel of Love* (side two)
Matthew Sweet's *Girlfriend*

Reading books, particularly quality ventures like *The Heartbreak Handbook,* is an excellent way to pass the time after a breakup. But, on this, the worst day of days, we prefer a more mindless form of escapism. Movies. Try these on for sighs.

videos for the heartbroken

other doomed loves:

West Side Story
Butterfield 8

Love Story
Terms of Endearment
Sophie's Choice
Mildred Pierce
Dangerous Liaisons
The Rose
The Way We Were
Sid and Nancy
Drugstore Cowboy

Revenge is sweet:

She-Devil
Revenge of the Stepford Wives (Don Johnson is in this!)
The Witches of Eastwick
House of Games
Thelma and Louise
Fatal Attraction and *Play Misty For Me*
Carrie
9 to 5

Must avoids:

•Any movie you saw with him
•Any movie with an actor that reminds you of him
•Any too-cute romantic fairy tale like *Pretty Woman* or *The Princess Bride* or *Beauty and the Beast*
•Anything with Jill Clayburgh

4

Break/Counterbreak

CONGRATULATIONS. YOU'VE weathered those first awful twenty-four hours — we knew you could. And now that your initial breakup shock has dissipated a bit, you're beginning to ask some of the more technical breakup questions, like, how will you get your stuff back? (See chapter 7.) Or, is he really suffering — and if so, how much? (See chapter 6.) Or, will you ever date again? (See chapter 5 — god, we're thorough.) Most of all, though, you want to know: *What horrible lies is he telling people about us?* It's a small and petty concern, sure. But at this point, small and petty is the way to go.

Odds are, when it comes to breakup details, he's saying pretty much the same things you are. Sorry to disappoint. His tale of woe may be couched differently, but the basic plot still stands. Anything else — feelings, reactions, reflections, yadda, yadda — that may spew forth from his largely uncommunicative (read: male) mouth is stuff you've already heard. Stuff that he's said—or tried to relay to you in that peculiar (read: male) way of his—at least once already. The only difference is, now he's talking to his friends and family. The rat bastard actually has a sympathetic audience. And that's what really burns.

Don't let that fire consume you. If you're spending a lot of time worrying that he's kicking your name around, your fears are probably unfounded. When it comes to stories about their own lives, men usually err on the taciturn side. They tend not to obsess, analyze, and delve into minutiae as deeply as their more perceptive (read: compulsive) female counterparts. Often, a guy's idea of expressing his despair or guilt involves little more than grunting and crushing empty beer cans against his forehead. Soul-plunging in its own way, we suppose, but not terribly specific. So it's a good bet that you've released—and retained—a lot more details than he has.

Even if he has miraculously discovered English as a third language and is bad-mouthing you to no end, what difference does it make? In all fairness, you probably wouldn't be a good personal reference for him, either. Don't get us wrong—of course we're on *your* side—but finding and maintaining distance is an important part of heartbreak recovery. You have to keep in mind that what he says or does has no bearing on your misery. You have to realize that words, particularly angry ones, have little credibility. You have to stop allowing him any impact on your life.

Actually, you don't have to do anything. We both got through heartache without following our own advice and lived to tell. All of the above would probably be a good idea, though. Still, we realize that in the early blush of singlehood, it's nigh well impossible not to wonder what his story is. A little curiosity can be an agonizing (read: agonizing) thing. And since we always strive to indulge your wanton, prurient interests, we offer you here a few stories from both sides of the fence. Our objective is strictly scientific: to observe the gender differences of the language of lost love . . . with the added thrill of voyeurism, to boot. Furthermore—since we knew you wouldn't believe us—we thought we would try to prove to you that *his* tale of woe usually bears a striking resemblance to *hers*. But enough exposition. What follows are five great stories, ten great versions: Welcome to (maestro, some game-show theme music, please) The (Where Did the) Love (Go?) Connection.

Colleen, a twenty-five-year-old would-be writer, met James, twenty-six, a few years out of college when Colleen interviewed at the magazine where James worked. Instead of a job offer, she got a relationship. Great, except that when it was all over, after three years of hard work, there was no severance package, not even paid vacation days. Then again, a few thousand dollars can't buy love anyway.

"We had been going out two years," Colleen says, "and I moved to Boston to go to grad school. We had never really talked extensively about our future together, but I looked at this separation as a test for the relationship. I had a sense that things were too easy—I wanted to see how we'd do together if things got hard.

"We spent lots of weekends together. He would have been happy to have a simple, nice time, but I needed to discuss 'us.' I initiated a lot of 3 A.M. conversations. I was very emotional, and he was sort of emotionally deficient—although he did have respect for my emotions. His detachment gave him the upper hand in the relationship. Still, we were pretty happy; things didn't start getting tense until about four or five months later.

"In December, I had time off; I went to New York to stay with James. This particular visit wasn't planned—I wanted to visit friends as well as see him, but maybe he felt like I was there just for him. Things felt strained; I didn't feel like he was giving a lot. One morning, we went out to breakfast and started having a tense conversation about our vacation plans. He had a week off and I was free for a while. He was vague about what he was doing—when I pressed him, he said that he thought he might go away with a male friend of his.

"That was it. Something clicked—I realized that he didn't care. It was a real blow when he didn't want to spend his vacation with me. I said, 'I'm leaving.' I went back to his apartment and started packing.

"And then he totally broke down. He's not a very emotional person, but he cried and begged me to stay. I had a lot of stuff that I had kept in his apartment—clothes, pottery I had made—and I began to put it in boxes. He really wanted to send everything to me, but I didn't want his help. I was surprised at the show of feelings. I think it was the reality of my leaving that changed him dramatically. In a weird way, though, he seemed to understand how I felt.

"James put me on a train to Boston, got on the train with me, walked me to my seat. This was completely unlike him. When I got back, he called all the time; he was willing to come visit me—it was an incredible change. Before, he had practically refused to acknowledge me; now, he was falling all over himself to please me.

"The breakup lasted about ten days. The dynamic in the relationship had totally reversed: He'd keep calling, I'd keep telling him not to call. He asked me to see him for New Year's, and I agreed. That's when we got back together, at James's initiative. But part of me never went back. We had a lot of furious relationship talk, not really fights, and he became more attentive and flexible, less critical.

"Finally, on Memorial Day—our relationship seemed to be guided by major holidays—we broke up for good. Things had been fine day to day, but we didn't share the same values. We weren't positive forces in each other's lives. I came to see that he wasn't going to be the one. I woke up that morning and said, 'This isn't going to work out.' He seemed almost relieved. I expected some regret the second time, but at no point did he express any. It was surprisingly painful—I don't know why, since I was the one who ended it. We were very amicable, though, very civil. I went back to Baltimore that day and never saw him again."

As for James's side of the story, it goes something like this:

"When Colleen and I first met," he says, "she was undirected and didn't know what she wanted to do with her life. At first I thought it was this bohemian thing; it was cool that she wasn't playing the game. I thought things would change and that she would get her act together. But she never really found something that made her happy. It became really frustrating because she couldn't do anything unless she had unconditional support from me. I felt like she believed that the relationship's success was crucial to her own success, so if things didn't work out for her, she could blame me. I guess that any problems we had existed right from the start; the relationship was diseased from the very beginning, but we got so used to it, we thought it was normal.

"We had been going out for about a year and a half when there was this five-month period when we went to about eight weddings. We saw all our friends getting married, and we began to think about our future—suddenly we were a couple, instead of a couple of people having fun. She got a wedding jones; she was afraid to say outright that she wanted to get married, but I thought it was on her mind. I stayed away from it. I thought if I offered her more closeness or commitment, I'd be throwing her a bone. And I felt pressured.

"I knew we were in trouble when she moved to Boston—I thought it was a way for her to get away from me. There were a lot of things in our relationship that she couldn't handle. She figured if she distanced herself from it, either she could deal with it or I'd have to make up my mind. In a way, the relationship ended when she moved away. After she left, we were in an epilogue stage—if I were a director, I'd say cut the last act.

"The first time we broke up, it was a real scene. She was off for Christmas break and came to New York for a weekend to surprise me. I was kind of cool to her; I hadn't expected to see her. We were at breakfast and I made some flip comment— I can't remember what it was—and she exploded. She went back to the apartment, told me she was leaving me. I went into 'Don't go, don't go' mode. I begged her not to do this. She insisted on packing up and then left a couple of hours later— after I had agreed to mail the boxes to her. I thought it was typical that even at the end, she was leaving me with an obligation, with one last thing to do for her.

"When she was gone, I was shattered. I was in tears. Three weeks later, we saw each other again, at my suggestion. I felt like I had to see her. I felt like even though it had to end, it couldn't end this way. We got back together for a few months; I think she thought I had learned a lesson, that the relationship would now be on her terms. With her, it was always a struggle for control.

"Things went on pretty smoothly that winter and spring. I think that the first breakup made us realize that we could break up and go on. I feel like if we had broken up for good the first time, we would have been wounded people. I think that we got to a point where the process of letting go was much more evolved, where we could let go of each other without feeling lost.

"The final breakup was supremely rational, friendly. I remember we were sitting on the beach on Memorial Day weekend, having a hopeless conversation about us. One of us—probably her—said that it was best if we didn't see each other. It was very mutual. We said stuff like let's be friends, it isn't that we don't love each other and it doesn't reflect badly on us—it just wasn't meant to be. We hugged good-bye at the train station. I felt good about it.

"I think that our relationship was one I should have had in college with someone. It was so much about both of us trying to figure out our identities. And I think that we didn't progress at the same rate and so a disequilibrium set in. In her script, I think she felt like she had tried her best to make things work and that it was my inadequacy that killed the relationship. She was blameless. Whatever. We kept in touch for a long time after it was over. We did see each other about a year later, and although it was fairly friendly, there really was the feeling that there was nothing left to say."

A pretty close approximation, if you ask us. Sure, there are a few missing links—most significantly, the fact that *he couldn't remember what he said that upset her to the point of leaving*—but hey, that Y chromosome can be a real memory blocker. Besides which, on the whole, James and Colleen are singing the same sad song. Maybe they just have different ways of hitting the high notes.

Allison and Michael, twenty-four and twenty respectively, were a similar case. They went out for two tumultuous years which finally came to a close when Allison moved in with, and then married, someone else (yep, that'll do it). As always, ladies first:

"Michael and I started as a one-night stand," Allison says, "but the sex was so great, we kept on going. We met when I had just graduated from college. He was younger than me—he had two years left of school, but he was taking a year off. I went to New York, and for that year, he decided to move in with me. I don't exactly remember inviting him. But when Michael makes up his mind, there's no easing him back.

"It was a good relationship in many ways—we really loved each other for a long time. But there were a lot of problems. First, I was almost four years older than him; I felt that the age difference was a problem, although he would never admit to it. He was a very heavy drinker. Sometimes when he was drunk, we would have these huge, blowout fights where he'd threaten to hit me. He never did—although sometimes he grabbed my arms so hard he left bruises. If he had hit me, though, I would have left him immediately. On top of all this, he always accused me of being 'a slave to my emotions.' It annoyed him. And he could never really commit to the relationship. I wasn't asking for marriage, but I wanted him to take the whole thing more seriously.

"The overriding issue, though, was deceit. His. Plus, he was a total slut. One weekend, he was invited to an ex-girlfriend's party and was planning to go without telling me about it. I found out because one of his friends slipped and asked me if I was going. Another time, he went out, got drunk, and didn't come home until four in the morning. He made up an outrageous story about hitting his head on a tree and passing out on the sidewalk. Right. It turned out that he had run into an old flame. All that lying really got to me.

"The anxiety of being with him got to be too much for me. After about a year and a half of him lying and trying to control me and not wanting to commit, I said I wanted to date other people. He didn't like it, but he said okay. Fine. The next night, though, he called in a drunken stupor and said there was no way he could deal with me going out with other men. I said then that we should break up. And I meant it. I finally wanted it to be over. But he couldn't accept that.

"I started dating someone else shortly after, and Mike was furious. He kept chasing after me—and although I didn't want to get back together with him, I let him persist. I still cared for him, but he was too extreme, too hard-line. I moved in with my new boyfriend. I felt bad that Michael was still so unhappy about it, but I did what I had to do."

And now, over to you, Michael:

"For the first year and a half, Allison and I were totally devoted to each other," he says. "We played house for almost a year, and it was great. But when I went back to school, things started to sour. Once we weren't in constant contact with each other, we started to fight nonstop. She wanted a sense of permanence from me, a commitment. What she didn't real-ize—maybe because I never really said it—was that I never thought of the relationship as anything but permanent. I thought we were indestructible. And I never thought about the future because I always thought it would be there for us. I guess you could say I never thought, period.

"The fights escalated; they became crazy. We would scream and rail at each other. Once I hit her—I'm not sure why. I was drunk; I think I backhanded her. The funny thing is, I can't remember what we fought about. Usually, it was over little things: I forgot to call, or I was grumpy, or she was. I cheated on her a couple of times, but it was just friendly sex, nothing important. Allison became really jealous, though, and we had to go through months and months of her intense jealousy.

"One incident I clearly remember was when an old crush of mine invited me out for a drink. Allison said she wanted to come along with us; I said no. I told her I was just having a drink and I'd be back at ten. The truth was, I was still infatuated with this other girl, and I wanted to be alone with her. We had a drink, then we went back to her house; she invited me to stay over, but I said no. By the time I got home, it was one in the morning. Allison was waiting up for me—and she was furious. I had a clean conscience; I kept saying, 'What's wrong with you? I didn't sleep with her, and I could have.' I actually thought Allison was out of line for being so pissed. Looking back, I can't believe that I could have been so insensitive.

"Finally, one weekend, Allie said that she wanted to see other people. I thought she was kidding. I asked if she had anyone in mind, and she said she just wanted the freedom. That's when I knew she was serious. I said, 'Absolutely not; break up with me now, or work it out with me.' She called my bluff a week later and ended it.

"I was floored, terrified. I had lost my best friend. I tried to get her back; I kept promising to change, saying what she wanted to hear, telling her I would commit, but nothing worked. I didn't understand the concept of too late. I think I forced Allie to leave me by being uncommunicative, not paying attention to what was going on. I took advantage of her. I took her for granted. With every girlfriend since, I've tried to do things differently—and I think I have. It's because of her, though. She was my first real love."

Once again, we're presented with two pretty similar sides of the same coin. Allison and Michael seem to agree on the most basic aspects of the relationship: love, passion, jealousy, deception, infidelity, alcohol. You know, your basic recipe for romance. Of course, there are a few little contradictions: For example, did he hit her or didn't he? An odd point not to agree on. In any case, it's interesting to note that Michael portrays himself as more of a dirtbag than Allison ever does. In fact, it's kind of reassuring to see that men's perspectives advance as their hairlines recede. Or maybe that isn't so reassuring.

But on to Val and Mark. Never ones to conform, they offer stories that are a little more varied than the rest of our specimens. Let's not get ahead of ourselves, though. To recap Val's side of the saga:

VAL: I didn't want to break up with Mark, because . . .

ELLEN: . . . for some insane, inexplicable reason . . .

V: . . . I was in love with the little lug. He began to put distance between us. Even after an agreed-upon week hiatus and a long "relationship discussion" where we said we would work things out, things continued to disintegrate until we gradually unravelled to a, um, to a . . .

E: Frayed knot.

V: 'Fraid so. Finally, as you'll recall, after total radio silence on his part, I had to phone him and ask if he wanted to call it quits. He said he just wanted to be friends. In other words, *auf wiedersehn*, baby. He said he hadn't called because he didn't want to hurt me. And thanks to his warm sensitivity, I felt wildly hurt and plummeted into a vast depression that lasted six months.

E: Right. Well this is Mark's version. In his words: "Val was really emotional about stuff I didn't understand; she would have these mood swings about things I couldn't grasp. I think she needed a lot of attention, more emotional reinforcement than I could give her." Kind of hard to believe, huh?

V: Shut up. Go on.

E: He says: "I lost interest in the relationship as it went on— not because of anything she did, I just didn't want a really serious girlfriend. I had always just really wanted to be her friend, I never had intended to have an ongoing thing with her . . ."

V: Oh, yeah, which is why he asked to be set up with me, why he called me up ten times a day, why he stalked me like a goddamned bounty hunter.

E: ". . . and by the last six weeks, I was pretty uninterested. I wanted to get out, but it was hard to say that to her. It was even harder, though, to pretend to like the situation. It was a double-edged sword. I don't remember exactly how it ended. I think we were hanging out in my living room one night and I finally said that things weren't going well, that I thought it was best that we didn't see each other. We definitely broke up face-to-face . . ."

v: Lie! We were on the phone! *I* had to call *him* up!

e: ". . . and she was pretty understanding about it. She fought it at first, but I think she knew in her heart it was over. It was a pretty clean break . . ."

v: If you call half a year of stringing me along like a dead fish *clean*.

e: ". . . although she might have called once or twice at one in the morning, really drunk." Wait a minute, wait a minute. You did what? You actually called him? You got drunk and stooped to calling him in the middle of the night?

v: Get off your high horse, Miss Universe. Some of us actually succumb to mere mortal emotions every now and then.

e: So it seems. Then he says: "We didn't really see each other after the breakup. We gave each other back our stuff — pretty awkward — but that was it. We didn't sleep together or fool around afterward."

v: Oh yeah? Oh yeah? What about that drunken night three weeks after we broke up when he lured me to his house to hear a song he wrote about us? What about the day we went for a friendly little shopping excursion at The Gap and I ended up giving him a handjob in the dressing room?

e: Val! Do you have to say *handjob*? Anyway, he sums it up by saying: "I didn't want to hurt anyone. I thought I handled it okay. Things were only in a state of flux for a week — I felt like I kept the pain to a minimum."

Val sputters unintelligibly, unleashes a gaggle of profanities, and wraps up with a brief teary squall.

e: How come our dialogues always end with you crying?

It turns out that Val and Mark's breakup was the most Rashomon-esque of the bunch. Big shocker — put a writer with an out-of-work guitar player, and you're bound to get irregular results. While Val tries to pull herself together, let's move on to our fourth situation tragedy: Deena and Greg.

"Even though we only went out for six months," says Deena, thirty, "it was incredibly intense. We worked in the same office; he was an intern and was six years younger than me. I kind of seduced him, I guess. In the beginning, I was chasing him, but things evened out as time went on. There was real heat—he was passionate, and the sex was amazing.

"Things never went bad—we always got along, and he never did anything wrong. It was when he started to really like me that I got nervous and started to sabotage the relationship. I don't know, I guess it was a culmination of office disaster— I got fired—and my own neuroses. I felt like I was robbing him of his youth. I was skittish, inconsistent. Somehow, I was scared that I would lose part of myself by falling in love. I would sometimes say really horrible things; I would get mean and tell him I didn't want to see him anymore. But then I would be miserable without him and want to get back together again. I jerked him around. I was a jerk.

"About five months into the relationship, I got a call for a job interview in Miami. I asked him if he wanted to move to Miami with me, and he said no. I was okay with that. After I went down there, though, he decided he wanted to move. I didn't want him to, but I didn't know how to say no.

"He came down to visit a couple of weeks later and some-how, the whole situation exploded. First of all, my mother wouldn't let him stay in my apartment; she wanted him to stay in her house. She never liked him—she thought he was too young for me. Maybe he was, I don't know. I was hating my life. I was hating myself, really. One night, I just lost my mind. I basically said, 'I don't love you, I do not want you in my life, get out of here.' Something came over me; I was possessed. I told him to go home. It was the worst night of my life. At three in the morning, Greg's mother called me (he had called her and told her I had gone loco) and screamed at me. She told me I was psychotic. Maybe I was.

"He left the next day. Before his flight, he came to my office. I was wearing a black dress; I looked like death. He looked at me and said, 'This is not the end. We'll take it easy. We'll see what happens.' We went to breakfast, and when we were walking back from the diner, arm in arm, I thought, what's wrong with me? Last night I was trying to eject him forcibly from my life, and today I'm walking down the street with him, holding his arm. This is nuts.

"We kept in touch over the next few years. I saw him twice, went to New York and stayed with him. It was always comfortable and natural when I saw him, but I knew it wasn't meant to be. I knew that our lives were too different; too much time had passed. I loved him so much, but I had never been in love.

"Remembering it all makes me sad, even today. I still have a place in my heart for him. He was always so good to me. I was a really difficult girlfriend to have—and he made it seem so easy."

Call it a hunch, but the word *easy* is probably not one of the top ten (thousand) adjectives Greg, twenty-four, would choose to describe his experience. Here's his story:

"At first, I couldn't believe that Deena would ever be interested in me," he says. "I was an intern; I was so much younger and greener than her. We started out as friends, but she began to openly try and seduce me. She was extremely aggressive: On our first date, we went to a movie and she grabbed my hand as soon as the lights went out. On the second date, she invited herself over to my apartment to watch a video and started making out with me in the middle of it. The next night, she asked me to go over to her house. As soon as I walked in the door, she was all over me; she whipped off her panties and jumped on top of me. She loved sex. She used to whisper over and over, 'Tell me you love me' when we'd be in bed. At first it freaked me out, but after a few months, I got used to it. It was an incredible whirlwind—romantic, breathless, exciting. I didn't know what would happen next.

"In the beginning, I was a little reluctant to get sucked in. But then, slowly, the tide started to turn. It started when she got laid off at work. She became critical—she'd correct me or tell me how to hold my fork, stuff like that. She treated me like she was embarrassed by me. Her friends thought I was a little Long Island hick. I began to hear things about how I wasn't the first intern she had hooked up with, how she liked younger men. But human nature being what it is, the more she rejected me, the crazier I was for her.

"One day, she announced out of the blue that she was moving to Florida. I was shocked. I asked her what would happen to us. She said, 'I guess we'll have to break up.' I couldn't bear to lose her; she was the first woman I'd ever loved. I asked her if I could move down to Florida—she never said yes, but she wouldn't say no, either. I was beyond confused.

"Deena left a month later. In the days leading up to her departure, she became increasingly aloof. She still wanted sex, that was clear, but emotionally she sent mixed signals. Despite everything, she still wanted me to come see her. I decided to make the trip.

"It was a bad decision—the trip was a nightmare. Deena's mother, Myrna, ruled her with an iron fist. She insisted I stay in the family house, half an hour away from Deena's place. Myrna was a rich snob who thought I didn't make enough money—and didn't come from enough money. I went down to spend time with my girlfriend and instead spent most of it being abused by her mother.

"When I got to Deena's house, she answered the door in lingerie and all-out jumped me. Then she started acting cold. Again. She sent me back to her mother's house. The next morning, her mother served me moldy bread and yelled at me for wrinkling a bedspread. I fled for safety to Deena's apartment. But there was no respite: Deena chose this time to tell me she didn't love me—never had—and wanted to break up. There I was, in hostile territory, just dumped, with a non-refundable plane ticket that wouldn't take me home for another four days. We talked through the night, slept fitfully for a few hours before dawn, and then she left for work.

"I packed my bags. I went to Deena's office to say good-bye. She was wearing a black dress, as if she were mourning the relationship. We went to lunch and she was crying. She said that she loved me but wasn't in love with me—the standard line. I went straight to the airport, bought another plane ticket, and arrived in New York that evening, broken-hearted—and broke. We didn't talk for a year, and after that, I saw her a couple of times but never felt the same way about her. I was too angry."

Zounds. Isn't Florida supposed to be the Sunshine State? A nasty little session, to say the least. Still, despite all the emotional turmoil, Deena and Greg seem to agree on most of the finer points, right down to the black dress (good news, girls: He *does* notice what you're wearing). Even high, horrible drama didn't engender an unfair assessment of the situation.

Now for our last stop: Ellen and Jake. To refresh your memories, Ellen's version of their breakup reads something to the effect of . . .

ELLEN: In the end, we just couldn't seem to get along. He was exhausted and depressed; I, uh, sought refuge in the arms of others. He was moody; I was annoyingly chipper. We couldn't communicate to save our lives. After three years, our relationship just sort of fizzled out. It was sad, but we still loved each other. We still respected each other. We parted with great affection and, I hope, dignity. At least that's how I saw it. But what did the rat bastard have to say?

VAL: Pretty much the same thing. In fact, after a month and a half of calling him up and leaving about five hundred messages on his machine, you would think he could have given me a story that was a little more interesting.

E: I told you he would keep trying to put you off.

V: Well, he did. Much in the same way he kept putting your breakup off. He says: "I thought about breaking up with Ellen for the last year of the relationship, but it never seemed to be the right moment. Eventually, I just jumped in a cab and went to her place, unexpected."

E: Mmm, well, he told me he just happened to be taking a walk, but I'll let it slide.

V: Good girl. He goes on to say: "I felt like the relationship was doomed. But it was hard to let go because of the comfort of the familiar and the fear of the unknown. I knew it had to end; our interests, our lives were drifting further and further apart. Our being together wasn't fueled by emotion but by habit."

E: Very articulate. Maybe if he had been that articulate while we were still going out, we wouldn't have broken up.

V: Maybe, maybe not. On that subject, he says, "I used to think that there was something we could have done to save things, but by the end, I couldn't imagine how things could change."

E: The only thing Jake knew how to change was his clothes. Ten times a day.

V: Hey, that's what he said about you.

E: Don't you quote Jake to me like that.

v: Well then, don't digress. Anyway, about the actual breakup, he says: "I didn't make excuses or prepare a speech. I basically said, 'I can't go on.'"

E: More or less. What he actually said was, 'We have to talk,' and then he was suddenly struck dumb. I practically had to charade the rest of the conversation."

v: Whatever. He says: "I tried to work things out, but I didn't have the energy, my heart wasn't in it. We didn't want the same things. The physical attraction had faded. I was firm, straight, and honest. By the end of the conversation, we'd come to a clear understanding that it was over . . ."

E: Hold on, hold on, back up to the part about the physical attraction fading.

v: "In a way, the breakup was spontaneous, but we both knew it was coming. While we were still going out, she didn't want to believe it, but when it happened, she knew it was right."

E: Who gives a shit what was or wasn't right, what the hell does he mean, *the physical attraction had faded*?

v: "I never dated anyone but Ellen—that wouldn't have been a solution to our problems."

E: He didn't think we had *good sex*?

v: "The real problem was that I was dissatisfied with my position in life. To move to the next stage, I had to shed my old life."

E: He didn't think up against the refrigerator, under the piano, in the back of the station wagon was *good sex*?

v: "It was just hard to separate from Ellen because of all the memories and associations we shared."

E: Who the fuck is he, *Valentino*?

v: "But when we finally did it, we did it for good. We didn't do it half-assed; we didn't drag it on any longer than it already had."

E: Excuse me for ever thinking I could possibly know what

good sex might be; obviously I have no idea what *good sex* is.

v: "She was characteristically stoic at the end of our conversation. I went on a vacation to Greece a few weeks later. During the first half of the trip, I was very depressed; by the end of it, I was more optimistic about the future."

E: "Well, he certainly did a good job of *pretending* that he liked it. . . . I mean, *I* wasn't the one who slept through our sex life.

v: Jeez. Enough with the wounded ego. Just get over the sex thing already, wouldja please?

E: Make me.

v: Okay, how's this? He says: "Ellen is a wonderful girl. I still love her; I probably always will."

E: Yeah, like a *sister*.

v: "I was always proud of her and the things she did."

E: As long as they weren't of a *sexual nature*.

v: "We have wonderful memories; we had a great time together."

E: Except when we were *in bed.*

v: Oh honestly, El. These are all nice, loving things he's saying. What do you expect? There are always rocks in the quarry—you can't expect only gems.

E: Meaning . . . ?

v: Nothing really, I just like how it sounds.

Which brings us to the close of our little his-and-hers exploration of heartbreak tales. Hope it was good for you. Naturally, men and women reminisce somewhat differently, but by and large, they try to be fair to each other. Surprisingly, we found that both sexes make an honest effort to recreate the events as accurately as possible. And, as the old saying goes, in truth lies comfort. So now that you're assured that his version of truth closely resembles yours, take that small dose of solace with a glass of warm milk. Those of you who need a considerably larger dose (with several shots of hard liquor) should proceed directly to chapter 5. N.B.: We only supply advice. Bring your own booze.

5

Your Top Ten Questions about Heartbreak

Old Wives' Tale #1: The recovery period for a breakup is roughly half the length of the relationship. In other words, if you've just come out of a four-year romance, you can kiss the next two years good-bye. But if you were madly in love for only four months, gosh, you should be right as rain in eight short weeks.

Please. This half-life theory is bunk. Emily Dickinson pined after her mystery man all her life—and she never even talked to the guy. Who are these old wives, anyway? What do they know about heartache—they're *married*.

Call us unconventional, call us crazy (but never call us before noon on a Sunday)—we don't like to make timetables for our emotions. In the world of heartbreak, everyone ticks to the beat of a different clock. For instance, Val mourned her six-month stint with Mark for an additional six months. Ellen took the Berlitz route and bounced back from the Jake Years (three and a half of them) in a fleet couple of months. You can't schedule something as quixotic and unpredictable as human feeling—you've just got to let things happen when they happen. As a very, very, very wise woman once said (we think it was Ellen, but it was really Val), I've got my whole life planned—and I can't wait to see how it doesn't turn out.

Old Wives' Tale #2: If you had really wanted the relationship, you would have found a way to make it work.

In other words, it's all your fault. Right. And masturbation causes blindness, cheaters never prosper, and it's the thought that counts. (Could it be? Might these old wives actually be . . . our mothers?) Enough with all their canned, sanctimonious drivel; we're more interested in Real Life, thanks very much. Real Life Heartbreak calls for some good, solid nuts and bolts to tighten up the pain. We know. We've been there. And in our never-ending quest to make your misery more bearable than ours, we conducted an informal poll of fifty de-boyfriended women and, between the jagged sobs, managed to pull together their top ten questions about heartbreak. Read 'em and (try not to) weep.

1. Is my pain showing? Yup. Heartbreak has no mercy. It doesn't just cause emotional turmoil—why stop there?—it takes its physical toll, too. Some of the most common symptoms reported: heartbreak pimples, heartbreak stomach aches, heart-broken capillaries, heartbreak insomnia, heartbreak intestinal disorders, and heartbreak headaches. Not to mention that your eyes and nose are often so swollen from crying, you can barely see to assess the damage. And you thought the relationship was ugly.

Many of the women we spoke to had such wrenching physical reactions to their breakups that, had they been weaker creatures (say, men), they might not have lived to tell. As one twenty-eight-year-old management consultant described it, "Right after my last breakup, I lived in a shroud of sheer, raw physical pain. When you're so connected to someone and then the connection's broken, you feel as though a part of your body has been ripped off. Like you're missing a vital internal organ. I was overwhelmed by the enormity of bad feeling. I'd wake up in the middle of the night; my eyes would just fly open. I'd lie there, my eyes darting around the dark, and I'd feel so alone. My body rebelled against the stress: My skin, which is usually clear, broke out. My stomach was killing me. At that point, I wasn't even concerned about whether I'd ever have another boyfriend—that came later. I was just terrified that this horrible diseased sensation would never end." Another woman told us, "I had always had a regular twenty-eight-day cycle since I was fourteen—it was like clockwork. After the breakup, my cycle suddenly became erratic: fourteen days, twenty-one days, thirty-five days. It was weird; it was as though my body were going haywire along with my emotions."

For many of our mourning glories, the ravages of heartache were most apparent in their appetites. Several women said they didn't eat for a week and then "ate everything short of the wallpaper off the walls." For one book editor, "Eating was my biggest problem. Every time I sat down to eat, I felt nauseated. I'd have to talk myself through meals: Okay, you can take one more bite. Just take one more mouthful. I was pretty thin to begin with, so I couldn't afford to lose much weight. But if I didn't eat slowly, I would throw up. I was eating with friends a lot then, and that made it harder—they were watching me, monitoring every forkful. I became horribly gaunt. I was exhausted. I would spontaneously burst into tears—after a while I didn't know if it was because I missed my boyfriend or because I felt so damn awful. I can't think of another time in my life when I looked or felt worse."

For some women, the food fixation is lasting. "After my fiancé and I broke up, I couldn't eat," said a twenty-seven-year-old public relations manager. "I dropped ten pounds in a few weeks. When my appetite came back, I got paranoid that I'd regain the weight, so I cut all fat out of my diet. All of it. To this day, I don't touch the stuff; I only eat fruit, vegetables, and the like. Before the breakup, I never worried about my diet; I ate everything and never really gained weight. But after, I was obsessed. I also started exercising like crazy — the time I spent working out was the only time of the day that I didn't feel pain."

So, what's the deal? According to Dr. Lonnie Barbach, a San Francisco psychiatrist, "After a breakup, you can tend to feel out of control. Your bills may be coming in and you can't pay them. The tears might be flowing and you can't staunch them. But you can decide what you put in your mouth — you can control your eating. I can see how that would be an attractive alternative to uncertainty, but it's not a good one. When you see yourself fixating or obsessing with food, it's a pretty sure sign that there are some things in your life that need to be addressed. Recognize the obsession; monitor how often you focus on food and then find other things to fill your thoughts that better address the problem." A brief sermon, girls: Statistics show that a large number of eating disorders are crisis-inspired; many women try to take control of their lives by altering their food intake. So not only is the heartbreak diet unhealthy, it's wildly unoriginal. Who needs to be a statistic?

But enough preaching. It's not as though we don't understand the appetite-suppressant powers of depression ourselves: Post-Mark, Val subsisted mainly on a diet of coffee, vodka, and cigarettes. Post-Jake, Ellen dropped to a staggering ninety-eight pounds — even the Duchess of Kent wouldn't have approved. Our take on this weighty issue: For a week, do whatever the hell you want. If you want to try life in the fast lane, don't force yourself to eat. If a food fest makes you feel better, munch away. Then, after your seven days are over, stop and reassess. Being a perfect ten doesn't involve looking like either a sticklike number one or a big round number zero. So eat—or stop eating—already. Put your skewed food anxieties in the pantry; you've got better things to think about.

As for the rest of the wreckage, try to use a little common sense (not always easy to come by at an emotional nadir) to smooth out the rough patches. Stay clean: Wash your face, wash your hair, put cold compresses on your eyes. Ellen turned to Ivory soap and liberal applications of Clearasil to soothe her complexion woes. Val favored Tums and a heating pad for her gastric distress. Almost everyone we interviewed touted the virtues of an ice pack (cucumber slices and wet tea bags were close runners-up) for the puffiness after the bawl. Aspirin, cold compresses, and nice friends who'll give you back-rubs were also voted emotional first-aid requirements. One final note: Keep up the ablutions. We mean it. Don't forget the deodorant. Put on your favorite sexy/comfy outfit. Get a manicure. What the hell, get a pedicure. In other words, get a sartorial grip. As one woman said, "You're already monumentally depressed—why depress yourself even more every time you look in the mirror?"

2. Will I ever forget him? No, you won't, and every day will get worse until your life is a living hell. Feel better? Of course not. The truth is, you'll never forget him (why would you want to?), but in time, when you think of him—and you will—you'll be kind. By the grace of Godknowswhat, the human mind tends to have a convenient amnesia when it comes to painful events. If it didn't, women wouldn't go through the agony of childbirth more than once, children wouldn't get back on their bikes after their first tumble—and you might never know how great it can feel to fall in love again. Blessedly, though, just when you least expect it, the amnesia kicks in and the bad memories go dim. Because of this wonderful fact, there are great big families all over America, kids riding their bikes well into adulthood—and all sorts of romantic possibilities hovering right in front of you, waiting to be plucked. Yes, it's true.

In the beginning, everything will remind you of him— songs, movies, snatches of conversations, small dogs . . . fabric softener . . . dust. You'll think wistfully of how sweet he smelled when he was sleeping or the way he whistled in a minor key. This is painful, but normal. Like the memories, these sensory reminders will also fade. If you're interested, there are ways to speed the fading process along. For example, do not play "your song"—or any sad song, for that matter— more than five times in a single sitting. That's just needless punishment. "I used to lie on my bed and play that Bonnie Raitt song 'I Can't Make You Love Me' about a hundred times a day," one jilted twenty-nine-year-old attorney remembered. "I had some twisted desire to worsen the pain." Well, in a word: CutItOut. Also, you might be advised to avoid your old mutual stomping grounds and/or friends. Whatever you do, don't hunt down his friends and grill them for information. You probably won't get any good dirt—and besides, there's no dignity in it. Finally, he's out of your life, so get his things out of your house. Purge your wallet and your home of any photos. Change your sheets. Throw out his toothbrush. Then, cry yourself a little cry and take advantage of the extra closet space. Don't talk to him. Don't write to him. Don't attempt contact.

Most of all, don't rush yourself. Ellen didn't take down her gallery of pictures (Jake, Jake's family, Jake and his friends, Jake and Ellen, Jake and Ellen with a big bunch of people, more of Jake alone, Ellen alone but smiling because she's thinking of Jake) until two months after their split. Val held on to Mark's shirts—literally *held on to*—for a good three weeks. We realize that everything takes time. But hey, that's one thing you've got a lot of.

3. So what am I supposed to do with all this time? The question isn't what are you *supposed* to do, but what do you *want* to do. Short of lying prostrate in his doorway, almost anything goes. Most of the women we spoke to said that they found the greatest comfort in talking to friends. One twenty-five-year-old respondent didn't even draw the line at friends. "I talked about it constantly to anyone who would listen," she said. "I particularly sought out people who would tell me what I wanted to hear. I loved to hear stories about couples who broke up and then got back together. Strangers, friends of friends, would call me up and say, 'I hear you want to hear stories about reunited couples.'" Experts agree that women's propensity to create support systems for themselves is nothing but healthy. "Friends keep you from miring deeper and deeper in your imagination," says Dr. Barbach. "They can help put a cap on obsessions and keep you grounded. They also serve as mirrors to your own thoughts." Plus, they lend you clothes and buy you beers. We'll drink to that.

About three-quarters of our women also found comfort in going out. One thirty-one-year-old told us, "I went out every night—I couldn't bear to be alone in the apartment we had once shared. I also heard from our mutual friends that my ex was going out all the time to bars, clubs, on dates. That made me so upset, I felt like I had to keep up." Many of these women chose to rally with male friends. They found that it helped to have platonic male companionship (not to mention a steady, nonpressure date for parties) and that by going out, they could distract themselves and ultimately come home tired enough to fall asleep. All in all, painting the town red seemed to be a popular escape.

Some women, however, preferred to remain in their blue

period for a little longer. One twenty-nine-year-old ad exec sat at home and "wrote letters to people, made phone calls. I tried to keep my act together. But it was all I could do to go to work. I definitely didn't want to go out; my apartment was my sanctuary. I'd have friends over sometimes, but I wanted to stay home where I felt safe." Another woman, a thirty-one-year-old accountant, stayed home "for about six months. I didn't want to see other people; I couldn't be nice to any guys. I was also afraid to leave in case that would be the night that he called and begged me to come back." Many of our home-aloners made an exception for movies. "I went by myself," said one. "It was an escape for me. I didn't have to make chitchat or get dressed up; I could plunge into an alternate reality and get out of myself for a couple of hours."

As always, the choice is yours. What's good for the gander isn't always good for the other gander. So if you want to romp, romp wisely and carry a big condom. If you need a vacation from the world, take one. If you want to have company, don't be too proud to ask for it. If you want to be alone, tell people to get lost. It's your ball game — you make the call.

4. What should I tell people? It depends on the people. Obviously, you're going to want to talk — but when you choose the people you're going to talk to, choose wisely. Reserve the blab-all approach for your closest friends and family members; they'll love you no matter what. On the other end of the spectrum, spilling your guts to total strangers can sometimes be a good outlet, too. Said one twenty-seven-year-old physical therapist, "I used to love to go up to strange men in bars and say, 'My boyfriend and I just broke up; I'm feeling very vulnerable right now.' They couldn't have been sweeter to me — it was a great opening line." Another respondent, thirty, found comfort in the kindness of strangers via mass transit. "On one of my bad days, I was on a bus and found myself sitting next to a middle-aged woman who was doing one of those word-search puzzles," she said. "One of the words was *bunny*—his pet name for me—and I burst into tears. She turned to me and very nicely asked what was wrong. I told her—in great detail. She was so sympathetic and really made me feel better. I had been trying not to bore my friends with the same old story again and again, so it felt so good to have a new listener. I never saw her again, but she was a real angel of mercy."

Then there's the whole category of people who aren't really friends but kind of are. Take your office colleagues, for instance. With them, a little discretion is advised. Even if you occasionally socialize with fellow workers, you may want to avoid giving them a blow-by-blow account of your latest heartbreak. Do they really need to know about every midnight phone call you make? They've got work to do. What's more, half of these sympathetic colleagues might be vying for your job; don't make it easy for them to snatch it from emotionally unstable you.

As for your immediate boss, you're probably better off avoiding the topic entirely. "If she thinks you're a mess emotionally, she'll think you are professionally, too," said one twenty-seven-year-old journalist. "I learned that the hard way. I didn't say anything to anyone in my office for two weeks. Then I told people. Right after I did, my boss started to see little problems with my work, even though it hadn't really changed at all. But she kept looking for flaws, and a month later, she actually ordered me to see a shrink. The irony was that during the first two weeks when she didn't know—the worst two weeks of my life, probably—she kept telling me what a great job I was doing. But after she heard the news, she saw me differently. For her, the perception that I was falling apart became a reality."

One last argument for keeping your mouth shut on the job:

Those eight hours may turn out to be the only time you have to forget about him. So savor them. We recommend that you wait until you can talk about your breakup without tears welling up; make a calm, brief announcement; and then drop the subject entirely.

5. What did I do to deserve this? Well, there was that fat girl you made fun of in the third grade. And then there was the little incident when you stole a lipstick from Woolworth's. Not to mention all those impure thoughts and the time you ate a doughnut at Passover. Strike that (the old wives possessed our brains for one second there). You didn't do anything. Neither did he. The most basic rule of adult life: Shit happens. Flush it or bury it, but don't let the fecal finger of fate prod you into blame and self-hate.

A lot of the women we polled, however, found themselves mired in self-recrimination. About 70 percent of them spent a lot of time asking, where did I go wrong? "I knew that I drove him away," said a twenty-five-year-old subject, "and I spent a lot of time blaming myself. Two years later, I still think it was my fault. I thought of all the things I would have done differently. I prayed I'd get the chance." Another woman, twenty-six, also confessed to heaping on the mea culpas. "I don't even like to talk about it with my friends," she says. "I always feel like I'm the one who ruined the relationship, and I feel like a jerk telling everyone all the mistakes I made."

Or get this one: One twenty-eight-year-old woman we interviewed told us that she felt like such "low-down scum," she made huge posters of all the mean things he had ever said to her (some choice examples: "Who could ever love you?" "It's time to take off some of that weight") and hung them up all over her room. "I needed to remind myself of how bad I was," she says. "I was a masochist."

We'll say. The bottom line is, breakups are almost always

joint ventures—you could never be solely responsible for such a cataclysmic event. Besides which, maudlin self-pity and blame will get you nowhere. Fast. So don't beat yourself up— you're going to need all your strength in the weeks ahead.

6. Should I try to get him back? Practically every woman we talked to asked this question. Funny thing was, they didn't all mean the same thing. About three-quarters of them wanted to know whether they should attempt a reconciliation. The rest wondered whether they should attempt . . . revenge.

A tough call, on both counts. On the reconciliation front, there are some key questions to ask yourself: First off, do you really want this? Are you pursuing him because you love him, or because you're kind of used to having him around and you'd rather be with him than be alone? If your reason is the latter, you're just going to keep yourself from getting on with your life—and probably bust up a good deal of self-esteem in the bargain. One twenty-six-year-old woman told us how "the one thing I obsessed the most about was how I could get him back. I actually bought a book called *Getting Him Back* and kept it by my bed and read it every night. I knew it by heart; sometimes I would call up friends and read them passages from it. My mind was locked—I couldn't think or talk about anything else." Another woman said that she wouldn't flirt with anyone or accept any dates because "I just wanted to get him back. I was convinced that if I couldn't be with him, I didn't want to be with anyone. I totally cut myself off—and probably missed out on some things that would have made me happy." Think through your motives carefully. A little misguided obsession can turn into full-blown depression. Our advice: If your mission isn't in the name of true love, don't waste your time.

The next question: Was it really such a great relationship, or does it just seem like it was great because it's over? It's an odd, unproven scientific fact: A man gets approximately 44 percent more desirable the second he returns your key. "When my boyfriend and I broke up," said one twenty-seven-year-old grad student, "everything that seemed bad in the relationship magically became great. Before, I had hated that he spent so much time studying (he was in med school); now I loved the fact that he was becoming a doctor. His family was French and it used to bug me that he spoke French all the time; now I loved his European-ness. I thought, I'll never have that again; I'll always be plain old American. I was immersed in the classic postrelationship rose-tinted hindsight."

As we said before, it's human nature to want what you can't have. But actually pursuing it might not be such a good idea. "If he's interested, he'll come back," says Dr. Barbach. "It's better to do nothing than to try and force the issue. Back off. You don't need to beg—that's not a position you want to be in." So get off your knees, girls—it's time to stand on your own two feet.

As for the revenge aspect of this question, well, we would *never* go in for that sort of thing. Well, almost never. For more details, go directly to **The Avengers,** the special retribution portion of our program, at the end of this chapter.

7. Should I date? Golly, do you want to? Many of our respondents touted the virtues of recirculation in society. "I started going out on dates after about two weeks," said a twenty-eight-year-old television producer, "and it was a good way for me to get my mind off things. None of them turned out to be Mr. Right, but a couple were Mr. Right Now. It was nice for me to be with men who wanted to be with me, who were interested in me and paid a lot of attention to me. They made me feel desirable—I had felt sort of like a leper in the last months of my relationship—and they boosted my self-esteem." Similarly, one thirty-three-year-old woman said that after the fall, "I started dating an older, divorced man in my building. I wanted to have a guy, a crush, some interest that was easy and fun. And he was. He didn't want any major commitment, and I never thought of him as my boyfriend. It was just a fling—something exotic and full of intrigue. We'd meet at midnight, have sex for hours. He saw me as this hot young thing and he told me this a lot. That helped my ego; I was able to sort of graduate from going out with him to going out with friends, people my age. I eventually got excited to meet all the cute guys I could."

The majority of our early daters stressed the fact that they didn't look for another long-term relationship during this time, but merely diversion. "I wanted to be footloose, a wild, single girl," said one thirty-year-old. "I dated all kinds of men: waiters, cops, tourists—whoever caught my fancy. I wasn't looking to settle down; I was looking for fun." Which, in the Rebound Republic, seems to be the right attitude. Starting an emotionally loaded relationship right on the heels of a breakup can spell disaster. As one woman, twenty-six, told us, "I met my last boyfriend in a bar, two days after I had broken up with a boyfriend of three years. I was crying, and he walked over and started to comfort me. We plunged into a huge, heavy thing—it was instant love. And then, instant crisis. I threw myself into this new situation to fill the gaps, make myself feel better, but I never really addressed why the previous relationship hadn't worked and how I felt about it. Within a couple of weeks, the new guy and I were talking about marriage, kids. I realized that I didn't really even like him that much; I was still in love with my old boyfriend. I felt like I had stepped onto a runaway train. The whole thing exploded. One night, I just left him—he still hates me to this day."

How can you gauge if you're ready for the dating game? Easy. Imagine you're at a party or in a bar. You see a really cute guy. Mega-cute. Wait, isn't that *Mel Gibson*? He looks at you, ambles over, and smiles a slow smile, long as a river. Do you stand up a little taller and assume the classic "tit stance," (breasts *out*, stomach *in*, butt *in*, saucy little *head tilt*)? Do you feel a flutter of interest move down your spine? Are you compelled to show off a little, to banter and tantalize? Do you go into dazzle-mode? If so, you're probably game for some mingling with the opposite sex. On the other hand, are you at said party or bar simply because your meddlesome but well-meaning friends keep nagging you to "get out more"? Are you wearing sackcloth and ashes? Does Mel hold all the appeal of a cold baked potato? Then give this dating thing a rest for a couple of weeks until you feel up to it.

8. Will I always be alone? In the words of one (undoubtedly male) pundit, you're born alone, you live alone, and you die alone. Not a cheery thought. However, keep in mind that there's a huge distinction between being alone and being lonely. Society has created a Noah's Ark complex, making us believe that we can't be happy unless we're paired off. "Women have been brought up to believe that they're nothing if they're single," says Dr. Barbach. "Mothers ask their daughters, 'Is there anyone new in your life?' as opposed to, 'Is there anything new?' It's almost as if it doesn't matter what you achieve, as long as you're married. Men are more trained to worry about their careers; women are taught to obsess over their relationships." Raw deal, if you ask us. No one should need a man in order to feel legitimate. The fact is, you don't need sex, you don't need men. If you *want* these things, that's fine. What's not fine is convincing yourself that you're a failure without them.

8a. Yeah, yeah, yeah. But will I always be alone? Sorry, we were just trying to seem politically correct. Do you want to know what we really think? If you want to be alone, you'll be alone. When you're ready for a relationship, you'll have one. If you think you're ready and you're searching, searching, searching but you're still not coming up with anything, it's because your subconscious knows better.

If you won't listen to us, listen to Dr. Barbach. "There's definitely something you can call readiness when it comes to meeting someone new," she says. "And there's a lot you can do to get there—for example, therapy. But you can't always perceive readiness within yourself. I know a woman who wants nothing more than a relationship. She keeps saying, 'I'm ready now—so where is this guy?' The thing is, she's not ready. She has so many other areas to deal with—for one thing, she doesn't have any friends. She's unsure about her career. These life problems are part of the reason she can't get involved in a relationship. The point being, you're not necessarily ready, even if you think you are. But when you are— really are—you can make things happen."

Need more proof? Okay. One twenty-five-year-old woman we talked to told us how, after the end of a four-year relationship, she found herself going solo for a year. "I've never had trouble meeting guys," she said. "Not to be immodest, but I think I'm kind of pretty and smart and personable. For some reason, though, for a solid twelve months, I knocked myself out trying to find at least Mr. Remotely Right and came up dry. I was totally willing to settle, even though there was no reason I should have to. Then, just when I least expected it, when I stopped trying so hard, I became friends with a guy and it developed into an incredible relationship. In hindsight, I think that prior to meeting him, I just wasn't emotionally equipped for a meaningful interaction. I had to wait until the time was right. We're getting married next year."

Major puke sounds. But it's a true story. As someone once said (we think it was the Supremes, but maybe it was Cher), you can't hurry love. So why try?

• • •

9. When will I feel normal again? Will I ever feel like myself? What is normal, really? The Highland tribesmen of New Guinea think it's normal to wear a bone in one's nose. As for whether or not you'll ever feel like yourself, well, let's run a quick check: Put your right hand on your right leg. Squeeze. Same leg, no? Same hand. Same lovable you.

However, if, *normal* implies *happy* — and oh, we can only hope it does — then you should bear in mind that, even when you were blazing a trail for two, you weren't always a truly happy camper. And recovery from a bad camping trip takes time and patience. Within that time, your best bet is to figure out what and who make you feel secure and comfortable — yes, more *yourself*. As one thirty-four-year-old woman told us, "In the weeks following my breakup, I realized that there were certain friends of mine who, somehow, made the hours pass less painfully. I didn't want to be with people who would sit around and say, 'That jerk, he never deserved you.' I didn't feel like man-bashing. I couldn't bear the thought of being with crowds of friends who dragged me out all night long to 'live it up.' Live what up? I needed to figure out how to just live, period. I needed a little solace, some quiet company. So I sought out the people who could give me that. I screened out everything else. Instinctively, I did whatever I had to do to make it easier on myself." And you should, too.

10. Does he feel as bad as I do? Let's get this over with. How he's feeling has nothing to do with you. How you're feeling does. His life and his emotions aren't your concern — the only way to get over him is to stop thinking about him. Face the facts (Maestro, a little Christian Science Foundation ad music, please): The most important person in the whole wide world is you. But if you really need an answer, it's yes. How do we know? In two words: chapter 6.

to do and do not:
a guide to suffering

In this time of torture and mourning, you probably don't know what's good for you. Okay, maybe you know that eating a low-fat, high-fiber diet will lower your risk of colon cancer and that regular exercise will increase your life expectancy (and if you don't, put this down immediately and go buy yourself a newspaper). What we mean is that you're probably having trouble figuring out how to process and react to your disappointment or fear or sorrow or depression in a productive way. Some people (read: Val, in Ellen's opinion) have a tendency to execute highly dramatic, detailed plots of self-destruction that only serve to compound their problems. Others (read: Ellen, in Val's opinion) try unwisely to avoid and ignore their pain, thus never resolving any conflicts. Neither of these extremes are useful in any way. In fact, extremes in general aren't really a good idea unless you're a performance artist (aren't we all, though?) or the CEO of a very large company on the verge of a hostile takeover. Assuming you're not, you can still take measures to suffer right. Below, a list of suffering dos and don'ts. To keep things interesting, we've jumbled them up.

should you or shouldn't you . . . ?

1. Go—alone—to yours and his favorite restaurant and order a duplicate of your last meal there together.
2. Stay home every night and "think things over." Weep. Get caught up in the romance of playing the victim.
3. Sleep with his best friend and do something with him that you refused to do with your ex.
4. Call your ex every hour on the hour and alternate between

begging him to come back and hanging up the second he answers.

We'll pause here for a moment. Before you pick up the phone, all of the above entries are *don'ts*. You hear us? They might sound tempting, but resist. Otherwise, you could hate yourself in the morning.

5. Lie in bed at night and fantasize about the last incredible orgasm you had with him.
6. Take a shopping day off from work and buy yourself something pretty.
7. Spend lots of time with your guy friends and expound on why men are congenitally unable to get in touch with their emotions.
8. Be meaner than a junkyard dog to anyone who is unfortunate enough to cross your path.

Another pause to refresh. If you marked these *dos*, you're half right. Fantasy is good, yes, but not about him. He's out of your life — and out of your bed. It's the (harsh) truth. Shopping is fine, but only if you can afford it. Don't blow your savings in an effort to buy relief; you'll only feel a lot worse come rent time. Spending time with male friends is a good way to get back in sync for future romances, but you'll only piss them off with the all-men-are-pigs spiel, seeing as how they, themselves, are pigs — we mean men. As for the junkyard dog approach, being mean can help relieve tension. But choose wisely. We suggest that if you feel like abusing someone, make it a sibling, since he or she has a blood obligation to love you for life.

9. Plan a party with a female friend. Don't be too obvious about it, but stack the deck in your favor by inviting more men than women (entice the men to come to the party by telling them, "It'll be all single girls, honest.")
10. Think about how *that thing* he always made you do (going to heavy-metal concerts, rubbing his feet, being nice to his dumb-ass frat brothers, giving him blowjobs, whatever) is now a thing of the past.

11. Put on your skimpiest outfit and reddest lipstick and go out to your neighborhood bar with three male friends. When other men try to get near you, have your friends act like they're your personal bodyguards.

12. Write adolescent diatribes about him in the stalls of public bathrooms. Be sure to include his full name and phone number.

These are do's. Go ahead: Have your agony cake and eat it too, without gaining those unwanted pounds. Extensive research has found these activities to be fairly harmless, satisfying, and amusing. What's more, they provide immediate gratification. Which, come to think of it, is more than he could ever offer. So enjoy your suffering, dear readers. We sure enjoyed ours.

The Avengers

Romantic retaliation is a tricky thing. As someone once said (we think it was Alec Guinness, but maybe it was Martha Stewart), revenge is a dish that people of taste prefer to eat cold. We're not exactly sure what that means—we think it means something like it's better not to fly off the handle all hot-headed, but rather to seek vengeance in a cold, calculating, meticulous way. Case in point: A guy writes a bunch of love letters to a certain famous young woman, she never responds; after several days of cold, calculating, meticulous thinking, he goes out and shoots the president. Yeesh. All in all, we'd have to say we don't recommend this frigid dish when there are so many toastier, tastier items on the just-desserts menu.

Why? Well, for starters, revenge can sometimes boomerang and turn on you in the worst way (look what happened to the guy who shot the president). And any shrink will tell you that getting back at him might just be your way of getting him back—hating someone that intensely takes just as much energy and commitment as loving him. Healthier just to let go, no? Plus, exacting that pound of flesh rarely offers long-lasting satisfaction—in the words of one woman, "there was the immediate thrill of getting at him, but then it would fade and I would start trying to think of some other prank I could pull on him." Which brings us to another important point: Revenge has a nasty way of escalating. You get the initial high, it dies down, you try to chase the high, and before you know it, you're selling the movie rights to your life as a serial killer. Not to mention the fact that if you strike too hard, he might retaliate. It's something to bear in mind.

In short, as one sage woman told us, "You can't get ahead if you keep trying to get even." A truer lesson never spoken, and yet one, it seems, that many women have to find out for themselves. The fact is, we heard so many tales of recrimination, we felt pretty shook up—shook up that there should be so much bitterness in the world, that love could so quickly turn to hate . . . that we didn't think of these tactics ourselves. Nonetheless, here they are, submitted for your perusal. *Caveat dumptor.*

THE NEXT BEST THING TO BEING THERE

These days, many women choose to let their fingers do the stalking; they prefer to seek vindication without ever having to leave the comfort of their own homes. In other words, they make use of one of the cruelest instruments of modern times: the telephone.

Most of the women we spoke to went with the old standbys. Several sent pizzas ("I sent six different pizzas—from six different pizza places so it wouldn't look suspicious—to his house one Friday. I heard later through mutual friends that he had a girl there that night. My timing couldn't have been better.") Another woman chose to send an airport limo at dawn to her ex's house, every morning for a week. She told the driver to honk by his window persistently until he came out. "He could never fall asleep after he had been awakened," she said, "so I would be sure I was robbing him of his favorite, precious early-morning sleep hours." Still other cold callers signed their old flames up for book clubs, record clubs, health clubs, and the like.

On a more heinous front, one jilted girlfriend regularly called and canceled her old boyfriend's credit cards and cash cards. Another called every month to have his electricity, telephone, and cable services turned off. There were scores of women who called their ex's to (falsely) inform them that they had some horrible sexually transmitted disease or other. And for those who believe that the message is the medium, one woman had an actor-friend of hers leave a series of increasingly urgent homosexual advances on the machine of her former beloved (who was now living with a new girl), while another left messages for him at work that implied he was interviewing for jobs at other companies.

The upside: Crank calls are generally on the more harmless side of the payback scale—like mosquitoes, they're pesky and annoying, but rarely life-threatening. Telephone revenge comes cheap. You never have to come face to face with your victim. It's relatively easy to recruit your friends to be accomplices. And barring the perils of Caller I.D., you'll enjoy relative impunity. **The downside:** As one woman told us, "once you hang up the phone, you've still got . . . nothing. You don't get to see him react. The gratification factor is low." **Is it worth your while?** It's your call.

MALICE DOMESTIC

Then there were the women who chose to keep their vindictive endeavors close to home. First came those in the minor inconvenience category: Un-alphabetizing his CD and record collections, changing the numbers in his phone's memory, pouring rubber cement down the drains, and disposing of all the assorted remote controls. In the major inconvenience sector, right before her ex left for a two-week vacation, one woman hid a dozen eggs in various, strategic places around his house. When he came home, he was treated to the walloping stench of her disdain. And in the just-plain-vicious category, one woman made a habit of spraying cheap perfume in her allergic-to-everything ex's clean laundry when it was in the dryer (they both lived in the same building). Unfortunately for him, he also had a terrible sense of smell; when he took out his wash, he would break out in hideous hives, without having the slightest idea why.

Well. **The upside:** Once again, you don't have to travel too far to achieve that tit for tat. You can be sure that you're getting him where he lives. A man's home is his castle — and since you're familiar with the territory, you know exactly how to booby trap all the trick doors and hidden staircases. **The downside:** You're riding the cusp of breaking and entering; just because he broke your heart doesn't mean you want to break the law. What if that ornery doorman squeals on you? Plus, it's easy to forget in the heat of the moment that if you still have his keys, chances are good that he still has yours, too. **Is it worth your while?** Hard to say. Going back to his home might dredge up a whole wash of memories that could be hard to exorcise. Seeing his things may trigger the uncontrollable desire to see him. A blast from the too-recent past has the potential to blow you away — and then you're worse off than when you started.

· · ·

REVENGE ON WHEELS

For those women who hate to sit around the house, we discovered a brand of retribution that puts you in the driver's seat—for a little while, anyway. We're talking car trouble here, and among those who've tried it, it's purported to be one of the most satisfying methods on the long, dangerous road to revenge. To name some of the more mainstream tactics, a number of women opted to let air out of tires and/or spray shaving cream epithets on the windshield. Another woman filled all the car locks with Krazy Glue. And going one step further, one un-squeamish type let a shoebox of mice loose in the backseat.

The only moving violation we heard of was an incident in which a particularly crazed heartbreak victim was driving in her car when she spotted her ex riding his bike on the other side of the road. "I saw him and something snapped," she said. "I veered over with grim purpose, determined to hit him. He looked back, saw me, and started peddling, faster and faster. Still, I continued to bear down on him and I swear to God, I really would have mowed him down, but at the last minute I had to swerve to avoid hitting some Volkswagen that was coming toward me. For once, the Germans actually saved a Jew." Note: This woman is a trained psychopath. Do not try this at home.

So when it comes to revenge on wheels, **the upside:** You're pretty much guaranteed to drive him crazy. You always knew he loved that car more than he loved you—and now he's going to pay. Besides which, you don't have to sneak around his apartment building to gain access to the scene of crime—and you can carry out your program under the dark of night. **The downside:** In a word: Car alarm. Setting one of those babies off can scramble your brain for weeks to come. You also have to know where he parked first. Furthermore, keep in mind that vandalizing a guy's car is the ultimate offense; it's practically akin to insulting his mother (except that the car's got a better paint job). He's going to be hopping mad, so if one day your car spontaneously explodes, don't say we didn't warn you. **Is it worth your while?** Again, a tough choice. If you're really on a revenge mission, we'd say mess with his car before you break into his house—it's quicker, neater, and more anonymous. Try to think as coolly as your vendetta-crazed brain will let you: If he's parked directly in front of his apartment or next to a police or fire station, bide your time. In fact, bide your time in any case—you'd be amazed how much less tempting that little Honda Accord looks in a couple of weeks.

BODY OF EVIDENCE

A surprising number of retribution-seekers called upon natural resources in order to gain satisfaction. It's ingenious, sure, but even more, it's disgusting, so we'll try to run through this quickly.

One woman urinated in a bottle of balsamic vinegar on the night that her soon-to-be-ex was cooking a big dinner for his family (his father subsequently got sick). Another woman similarly let herself go in a bottle of shampoo. And while we can't really applaud these girls for their delicacy, we've sure got to marvel at their incredible aim.

Then there was the weepy wonder who decided to blow her nose in as many of her former beau's silk ties as she could find. The scissors-happy girl who gave herself a pubic trim all over his bed, his clean shirts, his newly dry-cleaned suits ("and you know how pubic hair twists its way into *everything*," she told us with satisfaction). The woman who let herself into her ex's home when he was out on a date and, after scattering a few tampons around the bathroom, left her mark with a big, wet, red ketchup stain in the middle of his bed—covered nicely with the comforter, of course. Naturally, his date discovered it—and there was a lot of explaining to do.

For us, the topper was the girl who had had it with her boyfriend's drunken binges—she was sick of the way he'd come home, slur out rude things at her, and then pass out. Who could blame her, really? The umpteenth time he did this, she waited until he was safely unconscious and then, after carefully positioning herself over him, she felt . . . moved to empty the contents of her bowel on his chest. Then she penned a succinct note ("I've taken all your shit, now you can take some of mine"), packed her things, and left.

Talk about Yankee ingenuity. **The upside:** With this technique, there's no need to buy expensive supplies—you've got everything you need right at your disposal. If you're looking to score gross points, you've got 'em. **The downside:** It's easy to make a mess, and revenge like this means you're willing to stoop pretty low. There's no turning back after making a statement like that, so you had better be damn sure you want him out of your life *forever*. **Is it worth your while?** If you can actually muster the behavior, then yes. It's vile. It's horrible and humiliating for him, but it's kind of humiliating for you, too. It requires a certain finesse. But if none of these factors strikes you as being particularly significant, hey, more power to you. No one's really getting hurt, so . . . do what you have to do.

SLEEPING WITH THE ENEMY
Last, but not least, there's the sex category, in which girls use their bodies in an attempt to attain emotional justice. Sounds like a no-win proposition already, doesn't it? Sometimes,

sometimes not. A number of women slept with their old boyfriends' best friends. One of these women even staged a little dinner à trois with her old boyfriend and his best friend, at which she broke the news to her ex. "In the beginning, they were both fighting over me," she says. "But midway through the meal, they somehow bonded and became better friends than ever, while they railed at me for being such a bitch. I thought, 'wait a minute, what's going on, this isn't going as planned.' Then again, when it comes to revenge, nothing ever does."

Another woman enlisted the help of her best friend in order to seek retribution. Her ex had historically made passes at her friend, so the two of them lured him to her apartment with promises of a threesome. Without taking their clothes off, they managed to disrobe him. "It was kind of an innocent menage," she says. "We just wanted to insure that he was hard and hurting. After about an hour, we flipped on the lights, threw his clothes at him, and told him to get out. By that point, he needed to come, bad. He pleaded and cajoled and we just laughed at him. We pointed fingers at him, told him how pathetic he was. He burst into tears and left. And even though some people would say 'you call that punishment?', we were satisfied. We had set out to humiliate him— and we did."

Finally, there were the tamperers—the women who injected lubricated condoms with everything from Ben-Gay to Ambesol to hot chili oil (all of our surgeons assured us that they were careful not to perforate the condom itself, just the surrounding package. Now *that's* safe revenge). One woman confessed to leaving an old diaphragm with a rip in it in her boyfriend's medicine cabinet. "I called him a few weeks later and told him that I was pregnant—I couldn't understand how it happened, could he check my diaphragm? He did, and sure enough, there was a big, gaping hole in it. He freaked. I told him I needed the money—about $800—and he reluctantly agreed to send it to me. About nine hours later, I was the proud owner of a bouncing baby stereo. And if it sounds cold-blooded, maybe it was—but the bastard owed me about a thousand dollars over the course of two years, and I figured this was the only way to get it back."

No up or downsides here—sex revenge is a highly personal decision. In fact, all revenge is. Choose wisely, dear readers, and choose well. *He knows where you live.*

6

How Men Suffer

Nightmare #1: You're sitting in your living room, burning votive candles, poring over photos of Him, and the phone rings. It's your best friend, telling you that she saw the ex-love of your life at a party, drinking, laughing — *laughing!* — flirting, high-fiving all over the place, celebrating his newfound freedom . . . oh, and one more thing, she hates to say it (sure she does), but boy, does he ever look great.

Nightmare #2: You're standing in your kitchen, burning votive candles, eating Chunky Monkey (His favorite), singing sad songs, and the phone rings. It's your best friend, letting you know that she saw your ex at a restaurant, snuggled up in a banquette with some blonde, acting all cozy and goofy with love, and by the way, she just has to say (with best friends like her, who needs syphilis) that this new girlfriend of his really is a knockout.

UberNightmare: You've actually managed to get out of the house long enough to run to the corner drugstore: You've had the flu for a week, your hair looks like the *Exxon Valdez* oil spill, and there's a rather remarkable cold sore blossoming on your lip. You're browsing through the votive candle aisle when you bump into your former flame, arm-in-arm with his new gymnast/model/Nobel Prize—winning girlfriend, at whom you can barely aim to spit since the light reflecting off of that *big fucking diamond on her finger* is practically blinding you.

Then you wake up.

Time out for a few seconds of deep breathing. Turn over, try to relax—it was only a hideous dream. At low points like these, when Satan possesses the imagination sector of your brain, it's easy to convince yourself that you're the only one who's hurting. That your ex has somehow emerged from this whole thing better, stronger, more desirable, and is having the time of his life. Well, the truth is—and we'll couch this as delicately as we can—*you're dead wrong.* Guess what? Men actually do have emotions, and they experience just as much pain and suffering as we do. Maybe even more. No, really, because they've got to factor in the added onus of appearing strong and silent when they're really crying on the inside. "Society frowns on men suffering," says Dr. Bonnie Eaker-Weil, author of *Adultery: The Forgivable Sin.* "Men are pressured to know how to fix things; if they can't, they feel like they're failures. They're not comfortable with being out of control and helpless. When they think they're losing their grip, they get angry with themselves. And so they don't allow themselves to grieve."

The poor dears. How ever do they manage to muddle through life crises with such squashed, underdeveloped emotions? We're glad you asked. We talked to about a million men (okay, fifty) and asked them how they said good-bye to love. We requested them to describe in graphic, excruciating detail how they coped—or didn't cope—with heartbreak. As we suspected, each one of our respondents reported significant post-breakup angst. Each admitted that, after She left, his life was undeniably altered in some way. "Men and women suffer in pretty much the same way," said one guy. "The only difference is, women cry. Men get drunk first, *then* cry, *then* hunt her down." Which is not as far from the truth as you might think. After poring over the findings of our informal survey, we've surmised that guys make five major pit stops en route to heartbreak. Sure, some guys might forgo a stop or two. Some guys might get lost along the way and—perish the thought of asking for directions—wander around for a while before they get back on the right track. But in general, this is the Via Dolorosa that they take. Gentlemen, start your engines . . .

1. The Great Escape

Stop number one for most men: In this stage, a man will deal with his problems by simply . . . not dealing. He'll do just about anything to distract himself from the sad topic at hand—e.g., if he thought that walking over hot coals might help him get his mind off things, he'd happily march right over them. "There's nothing like a good bungee jump to put things in perspective," said one thirty-four-year-old respondent. Whatever you say, Geronimo.

"Men have trouble with empathy and compassion," says Dr. Eaker-Weil. "They would rather do than feel. Often, instead of being sad, they get angry. They sublimate their feelings into work and sports. They don't talk, they just get busy. This is the best way they know to be brave and masculine, which is how they think they're expected to act."

So if women have to be persuaded to stop obsessing, and need to be pushed to go do something to distract themselves, men are quite the opposite. "When my fiancée and I called off our wedding," said one thirty-year-old attorney, "I turned into a compulsive. I had gained weight over the course of our five-year relationship, and I became obsessed with losing it. Every day—and I'm not kidding—I did six hundred stomach crunches and four hundred push-ups, half in the morning, half at night. Even if I came home drunk at three in the morning, even if a girl was there, I'd do them. I started riding my bike, maybe a hundred miles a week. I got a trainer. I lost thirty-five pounds. When I wasn't working out, I filled my time with working, dating, partying, going out with clients. I took a summer share. I did everything to stay out of the apartment; it reminded me too much of her."

Exercise, in fact, seemed to be the most popular diversion for the men we spoke to. "When she walked out the door," said one twenty-nine-year-old banker, "the first thing I did was hit the Soloflex." Several of our guys said they joined health clubs soon after their breakups. "I never was much for working out," said one, "but now I wanted an outlet for my aggressions, my hurt feelings. I wanted to create something to do and someplace to go. Signing up with a gym seemed to be the easiest refuge for me at the time."

Other men chose less extreme, and considerably less strenuous, measures. Many of our guys chose to leave the country—on vacation, that is. "Right before my girlfriend and I broke up, I took a job in another city," said one respondent, twenty-nine. "I had a couple of months in between jobs, so I took a trek to Nepal for a month. After that, I was completely preoccupied with packing, finding an apartment, moving. It wasn't until I settled down in my new home that I had time to think about how much I missed her." Another one of our interviewees, twenty-seven, took a two-week trip to the Caribbean. "I wanted a change of setting, new faces to look at," he said. "I needed to distract myself, but in the end, it turned out that I had a lot of time to think about what had happened. I frantically traveled from island to island, but she kept haunting me. I realized that there was no running away—wherever I was, she was."

For those guys who couldn't afford the high cost of air travel, going out was a popular alternative. "I went out almost every night with a bunch of guys I worked with," said a paralegal, twenty-six. "We went from bar to bar, flirting with women, getting drunk. For the first week, everyone bought me drinks. I guess that was their way of showing me that they were concerned. I concentrated on keeping moving—that way, I wouldn't have time to think about what had happened."

"Men are much more interested in interaction than intro-spection when they're together," says Dr. Eaker-Weil. "They rarely share and confide in each other—in a way, it's out of respect for privacy and space. Instead of talking about things, they like to go out and pretend nothing is wrong. Their way of showing sympathy is to keep the guy who's upset busy. Because of this, men don't validate each other's feelings. When they do talk, they try to offer solutions as opposed to just plain empathy."

Finally, many of our escape artists drowned their sorrows in pleasures of the flesh. Some of them turned to old girlfriends, what one guy sentimentally called "known entities." According to Dr. Eaker-Weil, "Often, men are prone to return to old flames because they seek a familiar woman, someone who will validate their emotions, who will comfort them and not judge them. They're looking for compassion."

Other guys went the complete-stranger route, trying to heal their sprained self-esteem with the balm of fleeting inti-macy. "The week after she left, I slept with about a dozen women," said a political consultant, twenty-seven. "I wanted to prove to myself that I was attractive to other women, that she wasn't the only woman in the world." Dr. Eaker-Weil calls this "a power thing. A man may feel compelled to try to control new women, to exploit them, in order to feel more in control of himself. He might be angry and in some way, he's trying to make other women pay for what he's gone through."

But don't freak out—even if your ex is on a rampage, he's not likely to find love or happiness or really anything except his own sorry petard between the sheets. None of the men we talked to felt particularly moved by their bedroom rebounds; for them it was sex as sport rather than pleasure. "Yeah, I slept with a bunch of girls in the first few weeks of being single," said a musician, twenty-six. "It didn't help me feel better or make me feel worse, though. I think that for a long time, I just didn't feel anything."

I just didn't feel anything. It's a familiar refrain when it comes to men and heartbreak. One that rather neatly brings us to our next way station:

2. Denial Limbo

"When my girlfriend and I ended it after two years," said a thirty-year-old pharmaceutical rep, "my first thought was, 'I'm free, I'm finally free.' For about a month, I went out like crazy. When people asked me if I was depressed about the breakup, I'd say something like, 'No, it was time for it to happen; it was for the best.' I sort of swaggered around, like none of it really mattered. I think I actually believed that I was happier. She tried to call me, to patch things up, but I blew her off. Then, six weeks later, the realization that she was gone slammed into me. Suddenly, nothing looked good. I was like, 'What could I have been thinking? How did I let this happen?' But by the time I got my act together, it was already three months after the fact. She had a new boyfriend. I was too late."

Ah, the classic tale of the guy who will deny everything.

What, him worry? Often overlapping with the escape portion of our program, heartbreak lag-time causes men to plunge immediately back into life, as though nothing ever happened. In fact, they actually believe for a while that nothing ever did happen. They convince themselves that they're better than ever before. And when they finally discover that they're not, the blow hits them doubly hard.

"When my girlfriend and I called it off, I thought I was glad it was over; the emotional fireworks were too exhausting, too much of a pain," said a twenty-eight-year-old architect. "In two days, I was in bed with another woman. I relished my freedom. My ex called, and I didn't return her phone calls. I figured that I must not have really loved her at all. I enjoyed dating, being single again. This went on for about a month. Then, one day, I was going through my desk and I found a bunch of old letters that she had written to me. She was a wonderful writer, incredibly romantic. The letters told the whole story of our relationship, start to finish. Suddenly, I missed her unbelievably. I called her, but by then she was angry because I had previously ignored her. I began to think about her all the time, even more than when we were together. When we had been going out, I had cheated on her, but now I couldn't even look at another woman. For the next six months, I was completely true and devoted to her. The only problem was, she wasn't my girlfriend anymore."

Talk about bad timing. "Men can have a hard time recognizing their suffering," says Dr. Eaker-Weil. "They think that losing a relationship isn't supposed to mean that much——if they weren't married or engaged, what difference does it make if it ended? But sooner or later, they realize that they can't keep dodging the issue. They can't keep running around it——it gets harder and harder to do that——and so they just have to go through it. And that's when the going gets tough."

So what happens after the big epiphany? More often than

not, deniers are wont to wander into an even more delightful place, something along the lines of:

3. The Slough of Despond

"Men," says Dr. Eaker-Weil, "are more pathetic than women [hey, *she* said it, not *us*]. They're like sad puppy dogs. There's no question that they suffer more than women do, because they don't deal with the conflict for so long that it festers and grows, and when they finally do acknowledge it, the suffering is that much more intense."

Well, many of our respondents could certainly back that up. Some of our stories from the male rueing class far exceeded the limits of reasonable pain. During this stage, the guys we interviewed seemed to have a marked propensity for self-destruction and self-punishment. Then again, G. Gordon Liddy was a man, so why are we so surprised?

"We broke up at the end of the summer," remembered a twenty-eight-year-old ad copywriter, "and it was agony. I felt like I had been ripped apart. I was a vegetable. A few nights later, a bunch of guys and I were supposed to throw a party together. I got an industrial-size tank of nitrous and made out with the tank all night; it was the only way I could get myself to laugh. Nothing mattered except her — and the misery I felt when I thought about her. I sat on my bed and listened to sad songs, read her letters over and over, replayed memories in my head. I smoked tons of pot and drank gallons of beer. In four months, I gained twenty pounds from beer drinking, without ever leaving my room. There was a trail of beer cans from my bed to the bathroom. The only time I ever went out of the house was to get cigarettes, beer, and porn magazines. I didn't even want to masturbate that much — I did it anyway, constantly — because I didn't feel a physical need for it. My soul hurt too much. One night, I was so depressed, I got into bed with a friend of mine—a guy; it wasn't sexual at all—and cried my eyes out. I slept there with him that night. I was desperate. I didn't know what I would do, I needed someone to be with me."

Not a pretty picture—but a pretty common one. "I regularly got drunk by noon," said a freelance graphic artist, thirty. "I sat around and watched television and talked on the phone. The drinking made me fall asleep; I did it so I could forget. Then I'd wake up at night and couldn't go back to sleep. I'd toss and turn. I couldn't eat. I lost a lot of weight. I never shaved; I showered two or three times a week. I went through about six months of feeling sorry for myself until I got so bored, so revolted by my own pathetic-ness, that I had to come out of it." Another, a thirty-five-year-old screenplay writer, remembered "wandering into the bathroom every now and then, looking into the mirror, and cutting off a random hank of hair. Looking back, maybe it was a clumsy, desperate attempt at self-improvement. Or maybe it was just self-destruction: I hated myself and I wanted to punish myself by looking as bad as possible."

All of our men cited "letting things slip" as a primary symptom of their misery at this time. "I couldn't believe that such a tumultuous thing could happen in my life and everything else would go on like normal," said one corporate lawyer, thirty-two. "I left things all over my apartment. I killed cacti by not watering them—and they don't need a lot of water. I didn't pay my bills, I didn't renew my lease, my license expired, my telephone was turned off, my car lease expired, my insurance expired, I destroyed my credit. I destroyed my life. The only relationship I had that I treated in a normal way was with my cleaning lady. She took care of me, she left me notes—it was a stable thing. The rest was minute by minute. It was hell. There was no method to my madness."

Apparently, wallowing can be a real time-consumer: Most of our guys had time for little else. "Right after we broke up, I went away to Europe," said a thirty-three-year-old architect. "When I returned, the first time I walked into the apartment, I felt like I was being stabbed; everything was populated by images of her. I watched *Death in Venice* on a movie channel every night for a week. I'd walk out onto my balcony—ten stories up—and have suicidal visions. I had come back to the States to work on a project, but after two weeks of total inactivity, I realized I had to tell my boss I couldn't do it. My boss, thank god, was cool about it. He said don't worry, and transferred me to a project in another city, where I wouldn't be so reminded of her. That experience was like breaking a fever. I knew that that was the worst it could ever get."

In this stage, guys also have a tendency to be once burned, thrice shy. They retreat like the tide when it comes to women, relationships, and intimacy. "At this point, men don't want to make contact with women at all," says Dr. Eaker-Weil. "They're angry or they're afraid. They took the risk—and to them it's a huge risk—of falling in love, and they lost. They aren't willing to put themselves on the line again." As one guy told us, "I wasn't in a relationship for two years after the breakup. I didn't trust myself not to hurt another girl. I was afraid that I was still angry, that I would take it out on her. I had already fallen off the horse once, so to speak; I just couldn't face getting back on again."

In any case, this period of time is usually the cruelest part of any male-strom. But wait, there's more. Because whilst wallowing, there was a distinct faction of men who found themselves taking a short, sharp trip into . . .

4. The Stalklands

No, we don't mean the crazed, murderous, headline-making kind of stalking that's all the rage these days. We mean a less violent type of safari in which your ex calls and hangs up as soon as you answer, or lurks around your apartment building to see if you're coming home alone, or tries repeatedly to pick up the messages on your answering machine, or leaves you flowers or writes plaintive missives declaring his love. Ah, but that would be impossible, you say. Men never do such silly things, do they?

Mais oui.

Once considered the pink, frilly domain of girly-girls, crank calls to an ex-loved one seem to be enjoying increasing popularity among the male of the species. Surprised? We sure were. But facts is facts: Over one-third of the men we surveyed confessed to letting their fingers do the stalking. Their reasons were many: "I accidentally dialed her number" (we're so sure), "I wanted to make sure she was okay, that she wasn't too destroyed" (ego, much?), and "I was bored" (ever hear of MTV?) numbered among them. Some less lame explanations included "I wanted to talk to her, but then I lost my nerve," "I wanted to see if she was out having a good time without me," and "I wanted to hear her voice." Okay, we'll allow those—no stone-throwers, we.

Some of our men took that extra step and coerced friends or relatives into doing the dirty deed for them. "I used to ask my sister to call my ex at home on weekend nights, ask for a fake name, and then apologize and say she had dialed the wrong number," said one thirty-year-old. "I would listen on another extension. After a couple of these, I got nervous that my sister's voice would be recognized, so I made her wrap a dish towel around the receiver to distort the sound. It was a miserable, complicated little business."

Others were not quite satisfied with the next best thing to being there. "I occasionally hung out at my old girlfriend's house late at night," said a thirty-one-year-old journalist. "I wanted to see if she was coming home with anyone. She had cheated on me with a friend of mine and I wanted to see if she was with him." One enterprising fellow even followed his ex on a date. "They were going to a concert; I put on a trench coat and sunglasses and walked behind them about half a block, ducking behind parked cars and trees. I don't know what I was looking for. I guess I was kind of crazed."

Somewhat less surreptitious were the guys who chose to do their haunting via FTD. "I left her a single red rose every day for a month," said an ad salesman, thirty. "I thought it would charm her into loving me again, but now I see that it just made me look like a spineless ass." A financial consultant admitted to writing shameless love letters, making gooey love-song tapes and leaving them with his ex's doorman every week. A marketing exec who traveled frequently sent postcards from every city he went to. And a musician composed Desperately Seeking Susan-esque personals and had them printed in his local paper's classified section.

Fortunately, these haunting expeditions rarely lasted too long. Even the most lovelorn guy eventually sees the absurdity in moonlighting as Inspector Clouseau or serenading a twelfth-story window. "I had to make one last-ditch effort to win her back," said one of our surveyed men. "It was more something I had to do for myself than for her. I didn't want to feel like I hadn't given it my best shot. Once I had, I could move on."

And so shall we move on, to the last leg of our little journey . . .

5. Whine Country

Oh, so *now* they're ready to talk. And talk and talk. It took a whole chapter of shilly-shallying around before our guys were primed enough to stop and look carefully at what had happened to them. If you've ever had a close, platonic male friend, you know that this stage of heartbreak recovery can be the most annoying—for you, that is. You could deal with Mr. Everything's Fine, and you had ample sympathy for Mr. Morose, although you secretly feared that he might have to change his name to Mr. Jack Daniels. You may have even helped Mr. Furtive make a crank phone call or two. But now you're faced with Mr. All My Feelings Are Public Domain, and suddenly your female friends (even the really bitchy one who can't stop telling you about how cute your ex has become) are looking awful good.

Well, stick around. It's a long, hard road to emotional awareness, especially for a guy. "It takes a long time for a man to allow himself to admit that he's depressed," says Dr. Eaker-Weil. "He doesn't want to accept the fact that he might have been dependent on someone else, particularly a woman. In a way, he's still fighting against the old dependency-on-mother thing. High emotion is more familiar to women; men repress anger and loneliness and sadness. It takes a while for them to truly grieve."

For most of our guys, arriving at this point was more of a quiet realization than a blinding-flash-of-light, huge-puff-of-smoke kind of thing. "Gradually, I just found that I didn't need to avoid my feelings anymore," said a twenty-seven-year-old grad student. "I eased up on the drinking, I stopped killing myself with work. The pace somehow slowed itself down. I thought about how it ended and tried to figure out my position. It was a quiet time for me—I didn't want to be with friends; I spent most nights alone, trying to rediscover my equilibrium."

Not all men evolve with quite this much ease, though. "After a couple of months," said a twenty-eight-year-old talent agent, "I got sick of going out all the time—going around with a bunch of guys to stupid bars, getting drunk, trying to talk to girls. It was pathetic. I hated it. It just made me more depressed. I started spending more and more time alone, taking walks by myself, wandering around like a tired traveler. Actually *thinking*. I was still obsessed with my ex-girlfriend, but over time—with the help of therapy—I was able to see that I wasn't a failure, that we had loved each other and now it was time to let it go. I didn't love the process, but I got something out of it."

Often men reach this point because there's nowhere else to go. "I was exhausted, physically and mentally," said a thirty-two-year-old graphic artist. "I couldn't punish myself anymore—I just couldn't take it. Fifty nights of getting blind drunk was about forty-eight nights too many. I was running myself into the ground and I needed a breather. It wasn't until I stopped my frenetic scramble that I found a way to face myself and her, and cope with the whole mess."

About one-third of the guys we surveyed said that this was the time that they first seriously considered therapy. And some even went into it. "At first I was reluctant," said one thirty-six-year-old television writer, "but I was at the end of my rope. It really turned my head around. Being in therapy forced me to examine not just what was wrong with the relationship, but what was wrong in my life. It shook me out of denial. I saw that I was acting out familial relationships with my ex-girlfriend, that I was ignoring my inner child, that I had been misunderstood and the breakup was a function of deep childhood traumas that I had repressed when I. . . ."

Okay, okay, okay. Give it a rest, Sigmund. Our point is that men, in their own agonizing way, certainly feel the aftershocks of love lost, just as achingly as women do. And although *far be it from us* to take pleasure in their pain, doesn't it make you feel a little better to know that you're not the only one crying in your soup? Sure it does. But enough about them. Back to the far more fascinating world of Us. Now that we're assured of the fact that they're just as wrecked as we are, it's time to check out some postbreakup mechanics, starting with A Guide to the Whole Ex-Mess (a.k.a. chapter 7).

he did/she did: lists for the lovelorn

First impressions, we've heard, are lasting. Keep that in mind for when you start dating again. But the issue at hand is first depressions—the one thing you did or felt immediately after the breakup. First depressions, we've heard, are fleeting. So fleeting that many of the people we interviewed had to dig aggressively into their memories to recall that first and, perhaps, most honest reaction to the horror before them. Our sources, bless their broken hearts, came through with some humdingers. But what was most enlightening to us was the difference in the way that men and women confront their newfound single status. All of which nicely serves to reinforce our separate-but-equal-suffering theory. Below, his-and-hers first depression lists from thirty of our willing pigeons. Recognize anyone?

HERS

1.

"I lay down flat on the floor and didn't move for about an hour."

2.

"On the walk home, I discovered three dollars in my pocket. I veered straight into a deli, bought two Budweiser tall boys, drank one while I was walking—what were they going to do, arrest me for drinking?—and then sat in my bedroom and drank the other."

3.

"I called my pothead friend and asked her to come over with a joint."

4.

"I called him and said I was sorry for whatever it was he thought I did wrong."

5.

"I called my sister."

6.

"I called my shrink."

7.

"I called my best friend."

8.

"I called in sick."

9.

"I rented *About Last Night* because I knew it would make me cry. I watched it twice in a row."

10.

"I bought a Louisiana Crunch Cake, ate the whole thing, and then cried about it."

11.

"I went to Bloomingdale's and spent $200 on a new pair of pants."

12.

"I sat down at my computer and typed out the sentence, 'With trepidation in my heart, I stare at the blank screen that is my life.' "

13.

"I called my mother, then wished I hadn't."

14.

"I swore off men for good."

15.

"I called all of my ex-boyfriends and asked them to tell me why we had broken up. It was masochistic, but I was in that kind of mood."

HIS

1.

"I cleaned up the pieces of the dish she threw at me."

2.

"I punched the wall, jammed one of my fingers, and spent the rest of the night in the emergency room, talking to a heroin addict."

3.

"I rechained and oiled my bike."

4.

"I ran a dozen miles. I only stopped because my nose started to bleed."

5.

"I called an ex-girlfriend who was happy to come over and let me suffer in her arms. Then I kicked her out."

6.

"I paid the check."

7.

"I acted out my aggressions. At least that's what my therapist said—I thought I just screwed some girl I picked up in a bar."

8.

"I went back to our apartment to make sure she didn't steal any of my stuff."

9.

"I watched TV."

10.

"I got on the subway and acted like one of those crazy people who make lewd and insulting comments to women."

11.

"I got in the car and drove."

12.

"I put down the phone and got back to balancing the company budget. I didn't stop balancing that budget for three days."

13.

"I went to the neighborhood bar and made all the regulars buy me a drink. I toasted her memory about twenty times that night."

14.

"I called my bachelor father. He said, 'Didn't I tell you this would happen?' "

15.

"I turned out all the lights, lay on my waterbed, and jerked off."

7

A Guide to the Whole Ex-Mess

THE BIG breakup wish didn't come true: He still walks the face of the earth. Your earth. As if that weren't bad enough, you know that sooner or later, you're going to have to see him—be it through chance meeting or planned rendezvous. The very idea of seeing your ex face-to-face rattles you to the bone. We know. Running into our own respective exes would verily jangle us to the cells in the molecules in the marrow of our bones in the hole in the bottom of the sea . . .

Whether you're new at this heartbreak gig or a seasoned professional (knock wood a thousand times), even the briefest ex-sighting can be a jarring experience. Close encounters with Mr. Wrong have a nasty way of making you cringe, cry, and hate yourself in the morning. They can cause one tiny word to ricochet around in your brain like a jai alai pelota: Why? *Why?* Why did I act like such a goon? Why did I spit when I talked? Why did I sleep with him? *Why was I ever born?*

There, there. We know. We've been there. Surprisingly, however, we've found that it is possible to overcome humiliation and survive an unsettling run-in with some modicum of dignity. In fact, on occasion, we've even emerged feeling better about the whole thing. No kidding. Below, six decrees of separation that can help you through the whole ex-mess— no whys or wherefores required.

1. The Dreaded Trade-off

Your diaphragm is at his house. You need it—or, at least, one of these days you will. And come to think of it, he's been whining about getting back his stupid Ginsu knife set. How to make the trade? Very carefully.

First off, meet at a neutral place, like a coffee shop. If you meet at one of your apartments, uncontrollable nostalgia may drive you to indulge in nonproductive activities (you know what we mean), which can lead to even more nonproductive misery. Look at Zoë, a twenty-five-year-old production assistant. When she and her former beau made arrangements for their postgame swap, they toyed with the notion of meeting in a restaurant but then opted for his place. Big mistake. Huge.

"The problem was, I was still so in love with him," she says. "All I could think about was how to get him back. I racked my brains over what to wear that night. I decided on a cute little miniskirt that I had worn on one of our early dates—the one where we did it in a diner bathroom. When he opened the door, he said, 'Nice skirt. That brings back memories.' I said, 'Good ones, I hope,' and he said, 'Great ones.' Well, that was pretty much all I needed. He went to change his shirt and I lunged for him, grabbing him from behind, kissing the nape of his neck, moaning and sighing. He had to struggle out of my clutches so he could turn and face me. His expression was one of shock and horror. I was flustered and apologetic; he laughed and made some joke about how he was irresistible.

"We sat down at his kitchen table and began to chat, to catch up on things. And then I snapped again. I got up out of my chair and tried to grope at him. He laughed nervously and ran to the other end of the apartment. I actually chased him in four full circles around his living room, hating myself but doing it anyway. On the last go-round, he grabbed his keys and ran out the front door. I went out after him, tackled him before he hit the first step, pinned him against the corridor wall, and kissed him full on the mouth. He flung me off with more force than was necessary and told me to get a grip. I did. We went to a bar and got a beer, and then he left. I never got my stuff back and he never got his. I couldn't face him after that. I'll always remember the look of contempt on his face; I can easily say that that was the most humiliating night of my life."

Even if you think you're a little more in control than Zoë—and please God, you are—it's never wise to underestimate the power of old memories. Don't lead yourself into temptation; take every precaution to make it a safe swap. If this means that you have to meet in the passing lane of the Autobahn in order to keep it moving, so be it.

Second, discuss briefly what items you'll return to him, and vice versa. Include everything he's requested (although you are under no obligation to give back any items that may have slipped his mind). Remember: The same rules apply to you, so make a careful inventory. This is your last chance. If you keep calling him he'll think you really want him, not your belongings. Even if it's true, there's no need to humiliate yourself this way.

In addition, don't put off until tomorrow what you can get back today. The more you procrastinate, the slimmer your chances are of recouping all your possessions. Case in point: After Shauna, a twenty-six-year-old publicist, broke up with her boyfriend, Parker, she swiftly packed her bags—all eight of them—and then made the tragic error of leaving them in Parker's apartment. "It was too much to carry," she says. "I thought I'd wait until I had access to a car so I could drive it all to my house. A couple of days later, I called him to tell him I would make a pickup in the next few weeks. He said, 'Yeah, you should get it out of here, eight bags take up a lot of room.' Another week went by, and when we spoke, he said, 'You know, I've still got six or seven bags of your stuff.' I unexpectedly had to go out of town for ten days, and when I got back, we talked and he said, 'There are about four bags here for you.' A month later, I still hadn't retrieved my things—and the number of bags had dwindled down to one or two. Finally, I phoned and said I was going to show up that evening. He said, 'I don't see the point; there's hardly anything here.' Meanwhile, I heard from people in the office that his new girlfriend was walking around in clothes and jewelry and accessories that sounded suspiciously like mine. It really pissed me off, but what could I do? If I hadn't dithered for so long, I wouldn't have given the creep the chance to screw me over like that."

Often, simple objects can transcend the earthly and take on a psychological significance of their own. One jilted guy we know let himself into his ex-fiancée's house without her prior knowledge and cleared all his stuff out. But he didn't stop there. He also confiscated gifts he had given to her, things they had purchased together, her engagement ring—he even went so far as to take food out of her refrigerator. For him, it wasn't the stuff, it was the (incredibly childish) principle of the thing.

With Marsha, a twenty-seven-year-old radio producer, and her boyfriend, Richie, "an ugly little night table became the fulcrum of our hostility," she says. "A night table, for Christ's sake. It wasn't even a nice one, it was this old, cheesy-looking

piece of furniture. He made a huge issue of it—but he refused
to come pick it up. He said I should bring it to him. He lived
about three hours away and I didn't have the time right away
to drive that far. One day, his mother actually called and said
that she was really pissed off, that she wanted him to have that
night table. So finally I loaded the stinking thing into the car,
drove through sleet and snow to drop it off, and then turned
around and drove back. He wanted me to stay the night, but
I said no. I realized that this was all just a power struggle on
his part. That as long as I kept the night table, he felt like he
had something over me. I never would have made the trip, but
I felt guilty for dumping him, so in a way I was doing penance.
Plus, I could finally eliminate the only remaining tie we had to
each other."

One last little addendum: Know when to cut your losses.
We suggest the $100 rule. If it's worth any less—and doesn't
have sentimental value—then try to forget about it. Buy
yourself a new, better one.

2. Sudden Debt

It's not called cold, hard cash for nothing. Discussions about
money are always awkward, even in the best of situations. In
the midst of breakup hell, financial dealings can be downright
brain-scrambling. If, however, one of you owes the other
money, clearing the books becomes a cruel necessity.

Here's the dilemma: When you think in terms of dollars and
cents, you somehow feel like you're reducing your relationship
to crass capitalist terms. What were once matters of the heart
have become an impersonal system of checks and balances. It's
all too weird and embarrassing. On the other hand, if he's
borrowed money from you, look, you want it back. And if you
were the one who incurred a debt, let's face it, you really

should honor it. But what if he doesn't have the money? Or you don't have the money? It's an ugly business.

Of course, the easiest way to deal with the situation is to let the loan slide. If you have sufficient funds and/or a particularly charitable spirit, you might want to drop the whole thing. "She had borrowed about a thousand dollars to pay some medical bills," says Martin, a thirty-one-year-old writer. "I knew she couldn't afford to pay me back; I didn't want to give her any added aggravation. Avoiding any extra conflict was worth more to me than the money."

If you can't afford to be quite that magnanimous, then make every attempt to do your accounting as quickly and painlessly as possible. If you're the debtor, write a check and immediately mail it to him. If you're the debtee, politely mention that you'd like him to reimburse you, and then keep your fingers crossed that he possesses at least the tiniest dram of human decency and will pay you back with minimal hassle. You might be surprised.

Then again, you might not. If relations between the two of you are stormy, the money in question can become so much ammunition in a twisted psychological war. The person who is owed may feel compelled to lord it over the other. The person who owes can withhold payment out of spite. And the payoff in a battle like this can be meager indeed.

"Stan owed me over a thousand dollars," says Randi, a twenty-six-year-old journalist. "He was unemployed, and so I lent him money to pay his bills. Every month, he got further and further in the hole. Then we broke up—I left him for a friend of his. He was livid, to put it mildly. He hated me; I guess I don't blame him. At first, I didn't ask him for the money. But after a while I really needed it. I started bugging him. In the beginning, he kept saying, 'Yeah, yeah, I'll send a check.' But as more time passed, he got ruder. Generally he was an honorable guy; it was so out of character for him to be a welsher. Evidently, I underestimated his rage. Finally, one day on the phone, I reminded him about his debt for the hundredth time. He said, 'You know what, Randi? You're never getting that money back. You'll never see it again. I don't have it. Even if I did, even if I won the fucking lottery, I wouldn't pay you a cent. Fuck you, fuck your new boyfriend, fuck your money—you're not ever getting anything from me. You do the shit you do, you pay for it.' "

There's no easy way out of a financial quagmire, so just try to remember: It's only money. It can't buy you love or health or happiness (well, okay, maybe it can *lead* to love or health or happiness, but it can't directly buy it, like from a store or anything). Again, we suggest the $100 rule; again, we remind you to cut your losses while the cutting's good.

3. Close Encounters

Now that it's finally over, you never want to see the ugly lug again. Sort of. Hey, he's history. More or less. That being the case, every time you venture outside the safety of your own home into dangerous territories like your old favorite restaurant, or the movie theater in his neighborhood, or any street in the Continental United States, you half hope and half dread that he might be there. Particularly if you live in close proximity to each other, every moment is charged with a terrifying anticipation. You keep an eye out for his car. You give yourself whiplash because you could've sworn you heard his laugh. You spot a guy in a bar who for one split second looks just like him and you're practically in the critical ward. Okay, it wasn't him this time. But what if it was? What if you bump into him?

"The first time I saw Russell, it was a couple months after we had broken up," says Lila, twenty-seven. "I was window shopping with a girlfriend. She said, 'There's Russell, there's Russell,' but I didn't believe her because everyone always thought they saw him when I was around. When I finally looked up, though, sure enough, there he was, sort of stupidly waving at me. I wanted to run away — I hated what I was wearing; my hair was frizzy. My friend said, 'You have to go over, he saw you'; she practically dragged me over to him. We stood in the middle of the street for about five minutes and all he kept saying was, 'It's so funny to bump into you like this.' He said it about a hundred times. I said, 'I'm so nervous,' and he laughed. We hugged, and then he said he'd call me. When he left, I cried. It was so weird to see him and not be with him. He didn't look happy. He was thin. I didn't feel like I wanted him, but I could hardly breathe from the shock of it all."

Lila's reactions were fairly typical ones: nervousness, shock, fear of bad hair. Granted, there are varying degrees of damage that can be wrought by unexpected contact with an old flame. The way we see it, there are three major ways to get singed. First-degree burn: The two of you run into each other — neither of you has an escort. Second-degree burn: You're in the middle of enjoying a quality date when he suddenly materializes and blows your high. Third-degree burn: You're alone, minding your own business, when you spot him walking toward you with some girl — so obviously a professional, and we don't mean the kind that requires a briefcase — hanging off his arm.

Besides eating your heart out, what should you do? First of all, regain your powers of speech. Smile. Make nice. Keep all exchanges neutral and brief, excuse yourself politely — and hightail it the hell out of there. If it's a first-degree encounter, consider yourself lucky. Sure, you'll experience the ordinary weirdness that's bound to occur whenever you're forced to make halting small talk with someone you used to see naked on a regular basis, but at least you're spared the embarrassment of having an audience. If the rendezvous qualifies for second-degree status, resist the urge to obsess over the encounter with your date—it's just not sexy. And in the case of a third-degree burn, do whatever you can do to maintain your composure and then rush home, cry if so moved, and douse yourself liberally with sympathy and whatever poison you choose. Repeat as necessary.

4. The Last Supper

Unless the relationship ended with venom extraordinaire, chances are good that the two of you will, at least once, plan to meet again. It's kind of masochistic, dredging up all those old feelings and whatnot, but we're talking about heartbreak, so any rules of logic go out the window with the bath water.

What's so wrong, you might ask, about casually meeting an old friend for a casual meal to casually discuss, you know, casual subjects like the weather or car alarms or socioeconomic restructuring in the new global marketplace, even? Other than sounding like a *total casual snore*, nothing, really. But the fact of the matter is that you and that guy across the table are not old friends. You're recent ex-lovers. We're not talking casual, we're talking casualties. And if you truly believe that the two of you are going to discuss socioeconomic whatever-that-thing-is, we've got a book to sell you, cheap. Would the restructuring of the global marketplace really merit those sweaty palms, that brand-new outfit, the hours of obsession? Hardly.

Of course, there's more than one way to skin an ex-cat. When Naomi, a twenty-eight-year-old ad salesperson, had her last supper, she was so worried about losing control and panicking that she planned the whole evening with alarming calculation. "I staged it to the point that I would be on the phone with another guy when Warren walked in to pick me up," she says. "I giggled a lot, and I didn't get off the phone in a hurry. Looking back, I suppose it was pretty obvious I was trying to make him jealous. I wore an extra-short skirt and a sheer top with a black bra underneath. I didn't want to do anything sexual, but I wanted him to think I did, so I could reject him later. I chose the restaurant—a small Italian place that I'd been going to for years. I had even coached the waiters to flirt with me through the entire meal.

"I wasn't looking for any major relationship discussion that night; I knew why we'd broken up. I just wanted to prove to him that I was cool, calm, and collected—the opposite of what he'd expect. I wanted to bother him with my together-ness. The conversation was very perfunctory, almost sicken-ingly impersonal. It was as if neither of us would give an inch. I was disappointed. I took it to mean one of two things: that he was really over me, or that he was playing the same game I was. Of course, I obsessed over that for months afterward. After dinner, we got in a cab and he dropped me off at my apartment building. He didn't ask to come up or kiss me good-bye. But just as I was opening the cab door, he said, 'Everyone thought we wouldn't make it through dinner with-out fooling around.' I said, 'I guess everyone was wrong,' and slammed the cab door in his face. It was rude, but it was the only moment of satisfaction that I could eke out of the entire night."

We've got to be honest with you: Naomi's approach leaves us cold. As you saw, it left her cold, too. A general rule of thumb: If you're out to humiliate the guy, stay in. What's the point? Everyone feels bad enough already—why make things worse? In situations such as these, schemers rarely prosper.

Then there's an alternate approach—the one where you set yourself up to be humiliated. We don't really recommend this one, either, but sometimes it just . . . happens. Enter Mallory, a twenty-five-year-old law student. Desperate to re-woo her attorney ex-boyfriend, Trent, she called him up and asked him out to dinner. "I would have done anything to get him back, and I pretty much told him this on the phone. We decided to meet at a restaurant which was fairly far from where both of us lived—he'd insisted on it, probably so we wouldn't be tempted to go to one of our homes. I wore jeans and a tank top—he always said he liked me best in casual clothes, so I figured I wouldn't go overboard.

"When I got there, he was sitting at a back table, drinking a beer. My heart pounded. I hadn't seen him in a couple of weeks and when I saw his face—well, I didn't know whether to cry with happiness or despair. So I cried anyway, through the entire meal. We barely talked, I was crying so hard; the waiter even asked if everything was all right. Trent sat there and handed me napkins. He looked really embarrassed. The few times I tried to say that I wanted him back, it came out in hiccups.

"I didn't touch my food. Trent managed to eat all his ribs and most of mine, too. At one point, he said, 'I had wanted to talk about our breakup, to talk about whether our reasons had been sound. But seeing you like this, I think we should just put the whole thing behind us.' He said he knew that I would be fine without him; I blubbered something like 'Of course I will,' and he laughed. We ended up getting in our respective cars and not even kissing good-bye. When I got home, I was so hungry that I wanted to slaughter my roommate and roast her over an open fire. I settled for a couple of pizzas."

Oh, Mallory. The moral here: Wait until you can keep your emotions in check before you plan a tryst. Sobbing uncontrollably through dinner doesn't make for particularly good conversation, nor is it helping your eyeliner any. It's true, you may think you've got yourself all under control and then the shock of seeing his (pookie-wookie) face can send you into a dither, but try to safeguard against this. Don't hash and rehash old relationship problems. Don't argue or accuse. If it can't be a pleasant get-together, don't get together.

Which is not to say that last suppers always have to be miserable experiences. Every now and then, couples can find a way to make peace, make conversation, and actually have a good time. Accordingly, once again, we turn to the life of . . .

ELLEN: Me.

VAL: And Jake.

E: Oh yeah, Jake; okay, him too.

V: So he calls and asks you if you want to have dinner . . .

E: And I agree, although I just have to say that I don't really understand why food is so central to relationships. Why a meal? Why dinner?

V: What's he supposed to say? "Hey El, let's meet at the baths"?

E: I don't know, I guess I just thought Jake would be more original than that.

V: Ah.

E: Anyway, we met for dinner. I felt pretty calm about the whole thing, although I remember asking everyone in the office what I should wear.

V: I'm sure I had a little input in that.

E: None whatsoever. I finally decided to wear a blue dress that I had worn during some of our happier moments. When he came to pick me up, we had to decide on a restaurant. As we struggled to agree on one of the thousand acceptable eateries in New York City, I suddenly remembered for a fleeting moment how indecisive he could be. Finally, we went for Italian.

V: A potentially messy choice.

E: Not if you order carefully. We drove uptown and couldn't find a parking spot. As we circled around the block, I felt my stomach tie up in a knot. Again, I had a moment of remembering how tense and explosive Jake could be when he was in the car and something didn't go right—another driver cut him off, or someone was going too slow, or whatever. I had a flash of "Oh yeah, *this* is why we broke up."

v: But then it passed.

E: Right. We sat down to dinner and, for about an hour, caught up on things: his family, my family, his work, my work, yadda, yadda, yadda. Then, we started talking about us.

v: Uh-oh.

E: No, it wasn't like that. I had some things I wanted to tell him, things I felt like I needed to say. Hard as it might be to believe, I hadn't been particularly kind in the last few months of our relationship; I had been frustrated with him and I'd acted like it. So I wanted to let him know that I had always loved him, that even though it may not have seemed like it, I thought he was great, that he was a good person, and that I would always care for him.

v: What did he say?

E: He said, "That means a lot to me, El." He looked kind of misty and adorable and then said that he felt the same way about me. Oh, stop with the gagging noise . . .

v: That wasn't a gagging noise, I was trying to choke back a sob.

E: Oh. So it was like an exit interview, in a way. He dropped me off and we gave each other a long hug good-bye. We both felt really good about it when it was over. That dinner sort of confirmed the rightness of our breakup, but also of our togetherness, if you know what I mean.

v: Overall, a good experience.

E: Very.

v: How is it that you have the nicest breakup in history, and then a neat, attractively wrapped postbreakup dinner? In an Italian restaurant, no less? How do you keep everything so tidy?

E: Genes, I guess.

V: Then I was obviously born with a disaster gene. Mark and I met at a bar a month after the breakup — which, mind you, happened over the phone. We had a few beers, we accidentally brushed against each other on the street, and then we went up to his apartment and therein began . . .

5. The Inevitable Reprise

V: He was drunk; I was drunker. We were sitting on his couch — the very couch that we had had our first make-out session on. He was strumming a new song he'd written, and I was flashing back to our first kiss. I was remembering it in soft focus with fuzzy edges. I smiled and he asked what was so funny. I said, "I'm just so happy. I'm just so happy."

E: Val. Val. Your eyes are glazing over.

V: Sorry. I was all dewy with reminiscing. My heart ached. I said to him, "I'm still incredibly attracted to you."

E: And he said — ?

V: He said, "I don't want to do anything you'll regret." I focused in on his green, green eyes and was undone. I said, "Let me worry about that." He leaned the guitar against the wall and we kissed. I felt so many emotions: sadness, mainly, but also desire. We did it right there on the couch. It wasn't very good. Evidently, my body was wiser than I was and tried its best to make entry a, um, dry and difficult process, if you know what I'm saying.

E: Yes, I think we do; thanks very much for your delicacy.

V: When he came, I looked into his eyes. They were lifeless. Maybe that's melodramatic. I'll just say I didn't see any love at all. I felt instant regret and betrayal, but I could only blame myself. I had made the first move and he'd given me

fair warning. I felt small and crumpled. Demoralized. Unwanted.

E: And you stayed the whole night anyway.

V: It was too late to go home. I cried after he fell asleep. In the
morning, he got up and said, "You can stay if you want."
I got all excited for a second. Then he said, "Until I get out
of the shower."

E: What a jerk.

V: I ran out while he was still in the bathroom. I left my socks,
I was in such a rush. I felt used, but I had brought it on
myself. I swore I would never do that again.

E: What, sleep with an ex?

V: No, leave cashmere socks at someone else's apartment. You
know how much those things cost?

E: Actually, yes, since they were mine.

We repeat: **The inevitable reprise.** Oh, sure, it starts out
innocently enough. You consent to a friendly dinner. One or
two (hundred) margaritas later, you're making out wildly in
the restaurant parking lot. The big question: Should you go
home with him and get oléd?

Ideally, no. As Val found out, sex with an ex is tricky at
best. Not that you're going to listen to us. We hardly listen to
us. With this in mind, we advise you to do it if you have to,
but protect yourself any which way you can. It's not easy
making love perched atop a twelve-piece set of emotional
baggage. We don't care how flexible you are.

We also don't care how much time has elapsed since the
breakup, or how involved you are with someone else, or how
you think you've managed to harden your heart to his charms.
Yes, yes, we know you're Superwoman. We are, too. But even
superhero status can't make you fully immune to the daze of
auld lang syne.

Petra, a twenty-seven-year-old financial strategist, waited

more than a year before she had a rerun with her former boyfriend. "I found out that he was working at a bar in my neighborhood," she says, "and I went to see him—just to say hi. We talked for a couple of hours and then I went home. It was about three in the morning and, I don't know, something possessed me to call him at the bar. I said I was calling to say good-night or to tell him that I was glad we'd had a chance to talk, some bullshit excuse. He asked if he could come over when his shift was over, and I agreed. I wasn't dating anyone at the time, and I guess that seeing him made me nostalgic for a time when I wasn't alone. I realized that I missed the male companionship. I still cared for him, but I certainly didn't want to have a relationship with him. I wasn't even that attracted to him. I guess I felt a need to connect with someone I used to be close to. And I wanted to know that he still wanted me.

"The sex was eh. It was clear that it was a mistake, even while we were doing it. He said all this stuff about how the best sex that he'd ever had was with me. He said he still fantasized about me. To tell you the truth, even though he was trying to be nice, he just ended up looking a little pathetic. Afterward, we rolled over and went to sleep and didn't really say much. In the morning, when he left, he said that he'd call. He never did. All of a sudden, I felt a fresh wallop of rejection. I felt worse than ever—I hadn't even been thinking of him, and now he was always on my mind. I hated him for hurting my feelings like that; I took it as another example of my inability to deal with men. To this day, I regret it."

Most of us do. And even the few women who don't feel regret still find that repeat sexual performances have insidious residual effects. Rita, a twenty-eight-year-old graduate student, was engaged to someone else when she hooked up again with Pierre, her college boyfriend. "We hadn't spoken for almost two years and then, on a whim, I called him on his birthday," she says. "We ended up talking for a long time, reminiscing, catching up on things. Around three in the morning, we agreed that he should come over. It would be our last hurrah before I got married.

"The sex we had that night was amazing; I'll remember it forever. Although our relationship had never worked, we always had had an incredible attraction to each other. I remember looking at him, registering how he smelled, how he tasted, the way he took off his clothes. I was probably collecting memories, struggling to retain everything I could about how his body felt. It was hard to let go afterward. I shouldn't have done it, but I wouldn't trade that night for anything."

Which is all very well and good, except for the fact that now Rita's married. And she's still calling Pierre. Six months after she betrothed, she also betrayed. What she thought would be the equivalent of a warm good-bye was instead a dangerous hello.

It's a common misconception: That One Last Time is just a way to shake hands and part ways. But once you feel his "hand" touch yours, it might unexpectedly become impossible to let go. There's no aphrodisiac like unattainability. Besides which, having sex with an ex has nothing to do with holding hands, it's about holding yourself hostage to old feelings. Once you've done it, you're left with nothing more than a wet spot and a million tiny seeds of doubt. You're best off avoiding the whole situation. Since you probably can't/won't, do your best to nip those seeds in the bud and put the whole unsavory episode behind you. Don't dwell on regrets or remorse—just close the book (not *this* book—your metaphorical relationship book) and move on.

6. Wed Alert

There you are, happy with your life, dating a lot, feeling thin, and then word comes down the grapevine: Your ex is getting married. How do you feel?

It depends. If you're still attached to him, it can be a pretty devastating little piece of news. "I found out through friends that he had gotten married to a woman he'd been dating for about six months," says Tori, a thirty-two-year-old magazine editor. "It hurt—bad. The reason we had broken up was because he didn't want to commit, and now there he was getting married. I felt like my brain was howling. I couldn't work, I couldn't think. I was furious—how could he do this? At the same time, I kept thinking, 'What's wrong with me? Why didn't he want to marry me? Why am I such a loser?' I got paranoid and hungry for commitment. I chased away guy after guy because I kept badgering them to commit to me. I was obsessed with proving to myself that someone would want me, but I kept coming up empty."

For women who had achieved a little more distance, the news about upcoming nuptials still rankled. "I saw the announcement in the paper," says Mia, a twenty-six-year-old art student. "I had no feelings for him; I was living with someone else at the time. Even so, when I saw the blurb in the paper, my stomach turned. It wasn't that I wanted to marry him, or even that I wanted to be married at all. It was more that I wished that he shouldn't have one minute of happiness in his life. You see, we'd had a really hostile breakup. I guess I was pissed that anything good should ever happen to him."

For others, ill will was more focused on the object of the ex's desires than on the ex himself. "When I heard that Tom was getting married, my first order of business was to find out everything I could about his fiancée," says Maria, thirty-one, a museum curator. "By asking friends and by seeing her picture in the paper, I learned that she was gorgeous and rich and, apparently, well educated. She was the kind of person whose name is mentioned in bold type in the society pages. I am not. I mean, I'm cute and upper-middle class, but everything I am or own, I've had to work for. Historically, Tom had always gone for glam girls; we'd always joked that I was his one and only 'normal' girlfriend. Funny, ha ha. For about a day, I was okay with it. Then the jealousy started. Was I not good enough because I didn't have what she had? Was I not good enough, period? That's when the anger started in. I scanned the society columns for her name, hoping that she had committed some inkworthy faux pas, hoping she'd gotten into a limo wreck, I don't know. Meanwhile, I was in a happy relationship, living with someone, mind you. But something about her getting him filled me with hostility and rage. I needed to hate someone—and I guess it was easier to hate some beautiful girl I didn't know than a guy I had once loved—albeit a guy with lousy taste in women."

This much anger seems excessive to us. And then there's Maude. A twenty-seven-year-old commercial banker, Maude found out that her ex was getting married and, on a whim, went to Bloomingdale's to check out their bridal registry. Once she had the list, she walked through the store to survey the expensive crystal and china selections. "And then something inside me snapped," she says. "Claiming to be the bride-to-be—we actually looked alike, which helped—I got a fresh listing sheet from the registry department and proceeded to change all of the items. I went real tacky—and it felt good. For once I acted on my anger, and to tell you the truth, I'm glad I did. He had been telling people how elegant and well-bred she was, how different she was from me. I thought, 'Let's see how composed and dignified she is when this shit starts showing up.' I just wish I could have been there to see her face when she opened the clown-faced alarm clocks and dog-head bubble-gum dispensers."

And then there's the First-Runner-Up complex. Basically, this is when you perennially find yourself the last girlfriend that a guy has before he meets the girl he marries. Teresa, a thirty-three-year-old magazine research chief, tells of how she was "passed over not once, not twice, but three times. The first time was annoying; the second time was sort of comic. But the third time it happened, I fell into a deep depression. My friends, in an effort to cheer me up, suggested I charge men to date me so that I could whip them into marriage material for the next girl. I laughed and seriously wondered if there was any money in it. And then I cracked. I couldn't accept that it was just coincidence. There had to be something unmarriable about me. What was it about me that sent men scurrying off to spend the rest of their lives with someone else? And we're not talking long recoveries here; they got engaged mere months after our respective breakups.

"I spent hours every day trying to figure out what the problem was. What a waste of time—all I ever came up with was that I was too motherly. Another thing I couldn't let go of was that all of these breakups were amicable. In each one, we had mutually agreed that we were in a rut and that it was time to move on. So I'd move on to the next guy (and we'd eventually split for the same reason), while the last guy would go and get married a few months later. The whole cycle was too depressing—I never imagined that I would end up being the eternal last girlfriend."

No one does. And ultimately, no one is. It might be hard, but you've got to figure that this is just a streak of weird, bad luck. Besides which, if he doesn't want to marry you, you don't want him anyway. In any case, whether you're feeling devastated or just plain annoyed, feel free to indulge fully in your emotions—but for a limited time only. Two weeks should be long enough to bitch, to moan, "Why her, why not me?", and to make your friends tell you that it won't last. Any longer, and you'll start to look pathetic. So pull yourself together and, difficult as it may be, locate a little perspective. Realize that what he does no longer matters to you. That his happiness doesn't detract from yours. And that his marriage has no bearing on your life. Then take a deep breath and ask yourself: Would I trade places with his bride-to-be? Answer yourself (honestly): Not in a million years.

8

Look Who's Dating

''TWO MONTHS had passed since Jim and I had broken up. I had done my share of grieving, and I was ready to get on with my life. I was excited to start dating again; how does that psalm go— I rejoiced like a strong man ready to run a race. Tons of people set me up on blind dates. And each and every guy was really great: cute, personable, successful. Although none of them were exactly right for me, many of them are still dear friends.

"I was having the time of my life, being a single girl, enjoying all the attention. Then, one night at a dinner party, I met Tripp. We flirted and he asked me out. The first date was unbelievable—we talked all night and really connected. The next day, he sent me a dozen roses. We saw each other almost every night after that. Before I knew what had happened, I had fallen into the most important relationship of my life. I loved being single, but I loved being with Tripp even more. Every day I wonder what terrific thing will happen with us next. Every morning I marvel over the promise the day holds."

—Brooke, twenty-nine

• • •

Please. We were born at night—but not last night. Little Miss Happy here obviously has a rich fantasy life, or else this "Tripp" she's seeing is a chemically induced one. Plus, what's the deal with all that Bible quoting? Clearly, she's a decoy.

The truth is, if you're even remotely based in reality, you know that postbreakup dating is never this rosy. There's way more freefloating insecurity, stomach-turning anxiety, big lemon-scented depilatory messes in the bathroom. There are a million complex issues that surround the whole thing: how you feel about your ex, how you feel about yourself, how you feel about gender role models and the whole ego/id thing— you catch our drift. Often, you can be in the middle of a date, performing all types of unspeakable acts (pretending you know what congressional term limits are, chewing with your mouth closed), and you'll think, how the hell did I get here? Frankly the whole process is exhausting. Forget exhausting— it's downright petrifying.

"When my five-year relationship ended," says Jo, a twenty-nine-year-old architect, "I was almost afraid to get over him, because I knew that meant I would have to start dating again. I hadn't been 'out there' since I was twenty-three. I didn't know what it was like. The idea was terrifying; whenever anyone mentioned the word *setup*, my mouth went dry. I was scared silly."

It almost doesn't seem fair. First you have to pick up the two or three million tiny shards of your heart, piece them back together, and super-glue them in place. Then you're expected to take the whole fragile mosaic, cup it in your trembling hands, and offer it up to someone else—with a smile. Better to keep it in the display case at home where nothing can happen to it, no?

No. Better to put yourself in a padded room than to swear off dating forever. Granted, it's a cruel and unusual ritual; if all the angst weren't for such a good cause (i.e., weekends *à deux*, steady sex), you wouldn't stand for it another minute. But it is. So you do. And while no amount of advice can completely ease the pain, wouldn't it help to hear about other people's experiences from the front, and know that you're not the only one going through all sorts of weird shit out there? *Bien sûr*. So here they are, the best of all your stories, loosely categorized but in no particular order of importance.

Dating in Numbers

In the confusion of heartbreak, many women opt for quantity over quality—the pain of heartbreak sends them on a wild dating spree. Why? For Astrid, a thirty-year-old writer, dating was "a drug that blotted out my pain." Karen, twenty-eight, a financial consultant, says, "I needed to be appreciated." And Sally, a twenty-six-year-old grad student, says she was trying "to fill a void." According to Dr. Judith Sills, a therapist in private practice, "it can be very reassuring for rebounding women to know that men find them sexually attractive—that other men actually exist, for that matter. It can make them feel like they have a tie to the outside world—and that they're wanted there."

In any case, all of the women in this category had a lot of sex, a lot of messed-up feelings, and a lot of sex—until something made them realize it was time to cease and desist. Maybe it was simply that they were clean tuckered out. Or, *just maybe*, they saw that all those gymnastics provided them with more pulled muscles than answers. "Few women report that having a lot of casual sex enhances their self-esteem in the long run," says Dr. Sills. "Very few talk about feeling good about themselves afterward. It just doesn't work for women; the hunger for reassurance gets offset later by feelings of regret and a shaky ego." While a brief whirlwind can give you a certain kind of high, as someone once said (we think it was Aesop, but maybe it was Mary Decker), slow and steady wins the race.

ASTRID

"When Gary and I split up, I dated like a madwoman. Dating became a drug that blotted out my pain. I found myself dating four or five guys at once. I don't know where they came from—I met them through friends, on blind dates, I recycled old boyfriends, turned friends into boyfriends—you name it. I went out with a different person every night of the week. I discovered that if I gave guys the message that I couldn't care less about them, they would swarm all over me; that selfishness in a woman is irresistible. If I were a man, I'd hate me. It was exhausting. I didn't have the energy or inclination to cultivate feelings or affection; I couldn't focus on any single one. I probably dated in bulk because I couldn't find anyone I particularly wanted.

"The first date I went out on, I slept with the guy and never saw him again. After that, it was all a blur. For a few months, they'd literally come and go. At one point, I was sleeping with four men at once. I was alternately proud and horrified. It was like, wow, look at me, I'm a wild woman. I have to admit that, for a while, it was interesting to get a perspective on various sex techniques. But then, I realized that I'd started to treat men like objects and not like human beings; they were just toys to me. I'd hear a male voice on my answering machine and I'd think, leave me the fuck alone. Then I'd go out with whomever it was anyway. I dehumanized them—and myself—along the way.

"Last month, I realized that I hadn't slept alone in six weeks. I knew I had to slow down. Now, I've stopped dating entirely. I don't even have prospects—I've gone cold turkey. I don't miss the sex at all: I think that after the breakup, I never really had any genuine feelings of lust or passion—I would just make the noises, turn them on and off at will. It's sad. I wish it didn't have to be like this. I wish I could be engaged to the perfect man, but there's no such thing."

KAREN

"When the relationship ended, my self-esteem was pretty shaken up. I've never been good at going out and meeting people on my own, so I went out on blind date after blind date. It was nerve-wracking, although I must say that after fifteen or twenty of them, I became really adept at making small talk. I hate small talk.

"I began to feel like I was trying to recruit clients by cold-calling them. I felt like showing up at the agreed-upon meeting place and saying, "So, you like?" I think I was so insecure at that point, I focused completely on whether they liked me, and not on whether I liked them. I needed to be appreciated. I was devastated if the guy in question didn't call me again, even if I thought he was a total loser. I gave more blowjobs in a month than I had in all my sexually active years put together. Again, blowjobs are the ultimate way of trying to please a man—I wanted to ingratiate myself to them, some way, any way, it didn't matter how. Now, the thought of me, on my knees in front of some schlemiel, trying to get him to pay attention to me, makes me want to gag. Pun intended.

"With every failed date, I sunk lower and lower. Finally a girlfriend said to me, 'Look, you don't need to do this, you're running yourself into the ground, give it a rest. Guys can smell desperation a mile off.' I hated her for saying it, but she was right. I stopped looking and trying so hard. It was lonely, but in retrospect, all that frantic dating was even lonelier."

SALLY

"Soon after Dean and I parted ways, I took a month's trip through Europe. I slept my way from country to country—it was like, 'If it's Tuesday, it must be Jean-Luc.' I could have written a book called *Europe on Five Condoms a Day*.

"Prior to that trip, I wasn't a terribly promiscuous person. But something snapped inside me; I was desperately lonely and trying to fill a void of some kind. If I couldn't be happy, at least I could act like I was happy. My brain was numb; my body was operating on autopilot. When I'd pack my bags to go to my next destination, I'd look at whoever was in my bed and feel . . . blank.

"I knew that all this sex wasn't the answer, but I figured I had to fill my time with something. In a way, I was trying to reassure myself that I was desirable, that someone would find something redeeming in me. It backfired: I got paranoid that people only wanted me for my body. That my vagina was the only worthwhile thing about me. I think I actually believed that for a while.

"Luckily, the trip finally ended. I didn't end up doing much sightseeing. When I got home, I went on a sexual strike. I stayed solo for about a month and then—slowly, prudently—ventured out into the world of dating. This time, I actually met some guys I liked and eventually started a relationship with one of them. I think that dating after a breakup is like dieting: If you go on some crazy crash diet, it doesn't do you any good and only hurts you in the long run. But if you have a little patience and do it gradually, it may take some time, but you'll get results."

Home Alone

If the idea of putting on something too tight and too short and being talked at and paid for by a perfect stranger makes you want to retch, you're not alone. Actually, you *are* alone, in your house, but you know what we mean. "I didn't go out with any guys for over a year," says Betsy, a thirty-one-year-old market analyst. "I was afraid of getting involved and then getting burned again. I figured I'd play it safe."

Of course it's natural to go on hiatus for a while after a big breakup—if you immediately launched into another life-soldering relationship, odds are it wouldn't work anyway. Everyone needs time to refuel. But no guys, no sex, no nothing for a *year?* Jeez. "The problem is, avoidance can become habit-forming," says Dr. Sills. "Romance has a certain risk element to it, but the risk—and the fear that goes along with it—increases as you have less and less romantic contact with men. It may be easier in the beginning just to hang out with your friends. But if you're avoiding men altogether, you sacrifice satisfaction for security. It's not that great a trade-off."

Not that there's anything wrong with being by yourself. Time alone can be a healthy, happy thing. But if you've stayed in seclusion for longer than an entire television season, maybe it's time to analyze your motives. Are you a recluse because it truly makes you feel serene and content? Do you feel like your one-woman life is a full and satisfying one? Or was it just a great year for TV? If so, far be it for us to barge in on your solitude. But sometimes there are darker reasons. Charlotte, thirty, says, "I wanted to be alone because I was heartbroken. . . . But I was heartbroken because I was alone. I couldn't break out of the cycle." Annika, twenty-seven, says she took a sabbatical from men for eighteen months because "I was angry. I hated men—I didn't think I should start a relationship with so much hostility pent up inside of me." And Donna, twenty-five, like many women, didn't date simply because "I was painfully shy. Every time I tried to talk to someone, I felt so gawky and stupid. I decided it was better to avoid situations than to completely embarrass myself time and time again."

Most of the time, the solitary confinement is temporary. Many of the women we spoke to came out of their cocoons on their own; others turned to friends, family, and therapists to coax them out of their isolation tanks. We say: Go with whatever works. Because while one is certainly not the loneliest number in the world (don't believe everything you hear in songs), doing a little addition every now and then doesn't hurt.

CHARLOTTE

"When he left me, I cut myself off from the outside world. I was obsessed with focusing on me and my misery. I turned off the phone, I never left the house (I'm self-employed), I didn't even watch TV or listen to the radio—it was too distracting, there was too much noise in my head already. I went so far as to cover up my mirrors; I didn't want to see another face. Besides, I was so swollen from crying all the time, it was too depressing to look at myself. I wrote compulsively in my journals—I chronicled every feeling, every fear. Looking back, I think the catharsis of doing that was the only thing that kept me from going nuts.

"Things were this extreme only for about two weeks. Then people started to worry—they left urgent messages on my machine—so I figured I had to make at least some contact. I spoke with my family and friends on the phone, but not at great length. The conversations were perfunctory, meaningless—just token gestures to let everyone know I was alive. If you can call it that. I still didn't leave my apartment much, only to buy necessities.

"As more and more time passed, my complete seclusion became the norm—it seemed weird even to think about socializing. My friends started to drop by unannounced, hoping they could persuade me to circulate a little. Most of the time, I wouldn't answer the buzzer; I didn't want any company. I wanted to be alone because I was heartbroken. But I was heartbroken because I was alone. I couldn't break out of the cycle. I had created my own weird little world—no one else was welcome.

"I don't know how long this would have gone on, but luckily, one evening, my super knocked on my door. He was this young, friendly guy; a couple of times, we had had coffee together down in my building's lobby. Well, he barged right in and barked, "Enough is enough. People are concerned about you. What kind of life is this for a pretty girl like you?" I was furious; I got all cold and condescending, but he paid no attention. Then, all of a sudden, it dawned on me that he had said that I was pretty. It felt kind of good. He said he wouldn't leave until I walked across the street with him to a pizza parlor. I went. Every night for a week, he knocked on my door with a plan of some sort. I couldn't stop him—he had access to the building. He eased me into the real world again. He never made any passes at me or anything—he had a serious girl-friend—he was just being a kind soul. He was my good Samaritan; thanks to him, I snapped out of my daze and started to live a normal life again."

ANNIKA

"Lance and I broke up because he had a nasty little infidelity problem. I didn't know this for two and a half years—and we lived together. I swear, I didn't have a clue. One day, he called and asked what I was doing for lunch; I told him I was going out with a client. Right before lunch, I realized that I had forgotten some paperwork at home; I ran to get it, and I found him in our bedroom with this little blonde college student who worked at the Haagen-Dazs around the corner. Can you believe? He had called to make sure I was busy for lunch, so he could be in the clear. It still burns me. Anyway, all this is to make the point that I was totally blindsided by the whole discovery that Lance was a lousy cheat. I found out later that he had been cheating on me ever since we'd met. And I was furious.

"Unfortunately, my fury wasn't limited to only Lance. I didn't realize this until about a month later, when I went out on my first date with a guy from my office. We went to dinner, and for some reason, I suddenly had this incredible hostility toward him. In the office we had always been perfectly amicable, but in the context of a date I hated him. It was completely irrational. I was totally contentious, a rabid bitch; I gave the poor guy such a hard time. He was kind of rattled by me, and I don't blame him. The next week, I apologized profusely; I explained that it wasn't him, it was me and all my angry feelings toward Lance. He was pretty nice about it, considering, but it was awkward between us for a long time.

"After that, I was scared. I knew now that I was angry. I hated men — and I didn't think I should even think of starting up a relationship with so much hostility pent up inside me. I was afraid of the damage I would incur. I boycotted all dating situations. I started seeing a therapist who helped me to understand that Lance's actions weren't an indication that I was deficient in any way. I was angry because he'd made me feel used. Duped. Inadequate. And I was comforting myself by thinking, 'It's not that I picked a lemon, it's that all men are like this.' Obviously, that's not the case — I can say that now. But it took me eighteen months — and $1,800 worth of therapy — to come to that realization."

DONNA

"I didn't go out for almost two years after Jeremy and I called it off. In the beginning, it was because I was feeling too blue to be charming and witty. But after a while, I really wanted to start dating again. I liked being in a relationship; I liked having a boyfriend. The only problem was, I didn't know how to do it.

"Jeremy and I had gone out for seven years — I met him my junior year in college, and we stayed together for another five years after graduation. I didn't know how to date. Whenever I went out to a party or something, I would be completely tongue-tied; I'd spill something or trip over myself and make an ass out of myself. I'd look at other girls who were flirting and laughing as if it were the easiest thing in the world, and I'd wonder, how the hell do they do it? What's wrong with me?

"When it came to members of the opposite sex, I had no experience outside of Jeremy. So now that I was single again, I became painfully shy. Every time I opened my mouth to say something to a guy, I felt so gawky and stupid. I figured it was better to avoid situations like that than to humiliate myself time and time again. I worked myself up into such a state that I became convinced that I was a total clod when it came to dating. I was practically man-phobic. My friends all thought that I didn't date because I still loved Jeremy, but that wasn't it at all. I was just too damn nervous.

"Who knows, maybe I'd still be dateless to this day, except for the fact that one Sunday morning, I saw a guy who lives on my block in the supermarket. We started chatting — I never gave it a second thought, because it was such a no-pressure setting. He was really outgoing and friendly and started calling and stopping by. We began as friends, but then it turned into something more. It worked because I wasn't trying so hard; once I removed all these expectations that I had of myself, I could act like a normal human being."

Bed Again

Let's say you've gotten over the Madonna/whore complex and now you've attained a comfortable level of dating. You've been going out with a couple of different guys, and then you meet one that—kind of, sort of, possibly, not really, maybe—isn't half-bad. You go out a few more times. One night, after an uncommonly jolly evening, he reaches out and pulls you toward him, and you see his face getting closer and closer, his lips making a funny O-shape. Neurons fire. This guy wants to mash.

Alarms go off in your head—you haven't kissed someone new in who knows how long. Or maybe you're not so addled by the thought of mere kissing—contact with his mouth, you can handle, but what about contact with the thing bobbing amiably about two and a half feet directly south? What if all this mashing leads to s-e-x? You're so used to doing it a certain way—what if that's not the way they do it anymore? You've got body anxiety. You've got sexually-transmitted-disease anxiety. You've got performance anxiety. Let's just say you're anxious.

The first time you have sex with someone new after a long, monogamous relationship, it can be a loaded experience. For Erin, a twenty-seven-year-old lawyer, "Having sex unleashed all this hostility and resentment inside me. The second we finished, I hated him." And for Jill, twenty-six, "I had gotten a sexually transmitted disease from my old boyfriend, and I didn't know how to tell the new guy I was dating. It was a nightmare."

"Sex in and of itself is weird," says Dr. Sills. "Sex for the first time after a breakup can be even weirder. It often reawakens a vulnerability that you forgot about—and it might take time to feel okay about doing it again." Just remember, the guys are as nervous as we are—and it's even worse for them, because their anxiety is palpable. Literally. So take a deep breath, close your eyes, and think of . . . nothing.

BETSY

"I got set up on a blind date with Silas—what a name—and I wasn't crazy about him, but I thought that I should push myself to get out and date more. On our third date, he tried to kiss me, but I couldn't do it; I hadn't kissed anyone but Hank, my ex, in five years. It felt too weird. He said it was okay, he understood, and when he got home, he called and said he wanted to spend more time with me and take it as slowly as I wanted. That made me feel good.

"We went out steadily for a couple more weeks. On our fifth or sixth date, we slept together. The sex was awful—I didn't know if this was normal or what, I was so inexperienced because Hank had been my first and only lover. I felt empty inside. It made me sad—I didn't love him. I hardly even liked him. I wanted closeness and company, and so I settled for him. I had wanted to get a body between me and Hank, to push him farther away, but when I actually did it, I felt like I had betrayed him in some way. Or at least that I had betrayed his memory. It sounds irrational and maybe it was, but that's how I reacted.

"We broke up a few months later. I didn't care; I never had any real affection for him. It was a distraction for me. In a way, it was my introduction into the world of modern relationships. I'm not sorry I did it; although it wasn't emotionally fulfilling, it was an experience. As stupid as it sounds, it broadened my horizons."

ERIN

"I felt extremely vulnerable the first time I had sex with Barry. I felt exposed; I was afraid I'd get hurt again. It was our third date and we had really gotten along; I figured, why not? My reasoning was that I had to get back in the saddle again sooner or later, and since I thought Barry was a good guy—not necessarily someone I'd want to be with forever, but good enough—I might as well go for it.

"The thing is, having sex unleashed all this hostility and resentment inside me. The second we finished, I hated him; I was annoyed at myself for doing it, for not liking him more. I was scared because I let someone get close enough to me to hurt me. It made me angry with my ex all over again—and I took out my anger on Barry. We kept going out, but then he started to get pathetic, begging me to admit that I cared about him. I wouldn't. The more he chased me, the worse I treated him. I started to insult him in public, to make fun of his hair and his clothes. Every night I would kick him out—I never let him sleep over. And he just kept coming back for more. It was as if I were possessed to keep beating on him. I don't understand why he stayed around. Finally I realized that this was so destructive. I was too stuck in the past and the resentment it dredged up in me. The relationship was doomed from the start."

JILL

"The breakup was pretty bad, but the worst part came at my biannual gynecological visit. I saw my doctor about a week after the split; she told me I had vaginal warts and that they were contagious. I started crying right there, with my feet in the stirrups. I'll skip the whole painful treatment part and just say that I was fucking horrified.

"So there I was: I had gotten a sexually transmitted disease from my old boyfriend, and I now didn't know how to explain it to Carl, the new guy I was dating. What a nightmare. I had shied away from any sort of sexual contact until I met Carl. I loved him on sight—he was a real Southern gentleman, so charming and gallant; he held doors open and treated me like a lady. All I could think of was how this lady had warts on her vaginal walls. It was awful.

"We dated for a long time and slept together almost right away. I never said a word, I just insisted that we use condoms. About six months into the whole thing, Carl said he wanted to stop with the rubbers—we trusted each other; we loved each other. It was the first time I heard Carl say the L-word. It killed me, but I felt like if he really trusted me, I owed it to him to tell him about the W-word. He was shocked. He was clearly grossed out. This wasn't something they prepared Southern gentlemen for down in Baton Rouge. He said it was all right, but he acted distant and weird. When he left the next morning, I wondered if I would ever hear from him again. I did. We got past the trauma and continued going out, a little older (hey, the experience aged me about ten years) and a little wiser."

So it continues. Upon a quick review of this chapter, we realize that it's easy to jump to the conclusion that sex and dating after a breakup are miserable, unrewarding endeavors. Not so. Granted, it can be a big hassle—it's never easy to sort through a jumble of emotions and gently loosen and discard old ties. Hey, just giving your old clothes to Goodwill can be an agonizing experience, and you weren't even (that) intimately involved with them. But like the little girl with the curl in the middle of her forehead, when dating is good, it's very, very good. And so you go on with it—warts and all.

how to make it happen

You haven't been on a date for as long as you can remember. Then again, you've been so busy working/talking on the phone/staring into space that you really haven't had a chance to meet the four available, straight, single men in your metropolitan area. Fair enough. But maybe it's time to stop making excuses and to ask yourself that crucial question: What am I waiting for?

We're not saying that getting a date is easy. But was getting a job so simple? Or finding an apartment? In any event, you'll be a lot happier if you make your own love life happen. As the old saying goes, if you want something done right, by gum, you've got to do it yourself. It's a simple fact. Trust us. Or better yet, get out there and see for yourself.

1. Talk first. Forget all that hooey about not speaking until spoken to. Men love being approached. And if you start the conversation, it's easier to walk away if you decide you don't really like the guy. So flex your jaw, stretch out your vocal cords, and try something like, "Don't I know you from the cinematographer's party?" Okay, maybe not that, but our point is that if you can just muster up a little chutzpah and eke out a few syllables, you can start the ball rolling.

2. Use your friends. Networking on the job is tacky at best; networking for dates, on the other hand, is not only acceptable but strongly encouraged. Just make sure that the friend is trustworthy; that she knows more about the person she's setting you up with than his age, alma mater, and hair color; and that after it's a done deal, she'll keep her fat nose out of your business.

3. Be clumsy (on purpose). What better way to meet someone than by spilling your drink on his lap? This way, you get to do all sorts of lovely things like apologizing profusely, swabbing him nice and dry (paper towels optional), or insisting that you take his pants to the dry cleaners right then and there. If you prefer a less dramatically liquid approach, you can "accidentally" brush against him at a crowded bar or trip past him on the stairs at a party. This is an effective way to get attention, gives him a free view of your saucy little ass, and will make you appear charmingly helpless and in need of rescue. He can find out the truth later.

4. Have props. It always helps to have a guaranteed conversation-starter. Our suggestions: a dog, a book, a quirky piece of jewelry, a funny hat, a pretty child (clearly not yours), a musical instrument. This way, he's got an excuse to approach you in a casual, nonthreatening way. You know how men do so love their excuses.

5. Go backless. No man can resist putting his hand on the sweet, soft curve of a woman's back. Plus, going bare-back is much more subtle than the low-cut, high-cut, whole-body-exposure look (although if that's your thing, then by all means, wear it in good health). Remember: Not all treats have to be skimpy, they just have to make you feel delicious. In the long run, your best policy is to pick out something flattering and wear it easily. Being comfortable in your own skin — and outfit — goes a long way toward making you irresistible.

6. Position yourself. Location, location, location: It isn't true just for real estate. One of the first rules of successful date-making is to be in the right place at the right time. How? Look around you. If the guys are crowded around the jukebox, well, isn't it uncanny how you have a quarter burning a hole in your pocket? If the shoeshine stand is filled to capacity, you just can't help but notice that your boots are looking mighty scuffed. Think logically. For example, if you're in a bar, there are three things every man will have to do in the course of the night: buy a drink, use the men's room, and leave. So pick a prime spot—be it the front door, the bathroom door, or the bar— and enjoy the view.

7. Talk last. Just as beginning a conversation can give you untold appeal (not to mention control), so can ending it. Why get left behind when you can do the leaving? So go ahead, jump to a conclusion—with any luck, it'll leave him wanting more. Say something like, "It was nice meeting you, but I have to go; my friends are waiting for me." If you like him, take his phone number. Tell him you'll call him sometime. And then, if you feel like it, do just that.

the male point of view

Since dating takes two—at the very least—wouldn't the ordeal be a lot less stressful if you were privy to the other party's hopes and fears? Natch. So, once again, all for you, we did one of our survey thangs and asked roughly fifty guys your top ten questions about dating—with emphasis on the rebound variety. Here's what they had to say.

1. I met a guy at a party and the two of us hit it off. How long will it take him to ask me out? Will he make the call himself or ask someone to arrange it for him?

Apparently, most men have the nerve—they just need a little time to get it up. Fifty-one percent of our respondents said they would call within the next two to four days. The next biggest group—25 percent—claimed they would pop the question by the end of the evening; one (over)eager suitor said he "could barely wait until the end of the conversation." And the remaining 24 percent said they would hold off for an entire week, the objective of one of them being "to make the girl squirm." How sweet.

As for arranging the rendezvous, only two of the guys surveyed said they would allow an outside party to broker the date. The rest were all but horrified at the notion of being set up. Said one shocked respondent, "If you have to ask someone to do it for you, you don't deserve to go out with her in the first place." He's got a point there.

2. What does he consider to be a good first date? Does he feel pressured to make the plans?

Sharpen your forks, girls. Eighty-five percent of these guys want to take you to dinner—so even if the evening is a bust, you'll get a meal out of it. Half of that 85 percent said they'd make the invitation for drinks and, as one of them said, "If it went well, I'd casually suggest that we get something to eat." Talk about fear of commitment. A few romantic (read: cheap) sorts would prefer to cook the dinner themselves. Twenty percent said they'd throw in a movie (although many respondents thought that movies were a better choice for the second date), and the rest said they'd follow up with drinks, a ball game, a round of pool, dancing, you name it.

On the pressure front, 55 percent of our men said they'd feel no pressure to make the plans and that, in fact, they'd actually enjoy arranging the outing. Ten percent said they thought it would be their responsibility to make the plans for the night but wouldn't feel unduly stressed out about it. Meanwhile, back at the neurosis ranch, 35 percent said they'd agonize over and feel "burdened by the obligation" of trying to make your evening together a pleasure cruise.

3. Will he pick up the tab for the whole night? Should I offer money?

Here's where we separate the artistes from the M.B.A.s. Eighty percent assured us that they'd be happy to shell out the bucks—at least for the first date; the remaining 20 percent would choose to go Dutch. As for whether or not you should whip out your wallet, 70 percent of the guys said that "it would be a nice gesture" but "it wasn't really necessary"—and they'd refuse it anyway. The other 30 percent clearly stated that they would be annoyed if the girl didn't at least offer to pay her part—if not on the first date, then unquestionably on the second. Some, in fact, would be downright pissed if, in this enlightened day and age, the woman didn't front her share. As one indignant respondent fumed, "What, does she expect me to pay for the simple pleasure of her company?" In other words, if you want to make a good impression, don't forget the money, honey.

4. What makes him most anxious before the date?

We girls aren't the only ones with jangled nerves before a big night out—in our survey, guy anxiety raged. A charming 40 percent of our men fretted about whether "she'll like me as much as I like her." Isn't that special? Other worries included: the evening's plans, the possibility of boredom, the conversation, his looks, her looks, and expenses ("What if my Visa card gets denied?"). On the more bizarre end, some of our guys said they'd be stressed out over catching a sexually transmitted disease, getting into a car accident, or running into an ex-girlfriend.

5. What would make the date a success? A failure? What could a girl do to make the evening easier?

When it comes to guys' dating success stories, almost all the answers were only slight variations on a common theme. Our guys thought it would be a great night if they felt comfortable, enjoyed the conversation, felt attracted to the girl in question, felt as though they had connected with her in some way, and wanted to see her again. "I know it's been a success if I get a nice, long good-night kiss at the end of the evening," said one respondent. The guys would consider the night a flop, however, if they were bored, impatient for the date to end, and unmoved by their companion intellectually, sexually, or emotionally.

What can you do to keep the ball rolling? In a word, participate. "Things go much more smoothly if the girl gives you some input— if she has opinions and contributes to the evening's activities." Hear, hear. When it comes to the early stages of romance, good things hardly ever come to those who sit on their lazy behinds and wait.

6. What will he say at the end of the date if he's going to call again? What if he's not?

We suspected it all along: Whether a guy means it or not, he'll say those three little words: I'll call you. At least that's what 25 percent of the guys we polled said. The rest of them were more honest. "If I really want to see her again, I'll say something specific, like what are you doing next weekend, or I'll call you on Tuesday and we can make plans," said one respondent. "If I'm not interested, I try to keep it vague—thanks, I had a nice time, I'll talk to you sometime." And then there was the small percentage of men (5 percent) who would refuse to say they'd call, even if they planned to. Why? Who knows? Why the hell do they do anything anyway?

7. If he planned to call, how long would he wait? Would he be turned off if I called first?

Our basic rule of thumb: If he hasn't called in a week, you can pretty much write him off. Forty percent of our guys said they'd call in three days, about 35 percent said two days, and an ardently infatuated 23 percent said they'd call the next day. Only 2 percent said they'd wait longer than a week.

A whopping 90 percent said that they wouldn't be offended at all if the woman called first; on the contrary, most said that they'd be flattered. "I'd love it," said one guy. "She'd be at my mercy." Great, another Cro-Mag on the loose.

8. Are guys wary of women on the rebound?

From everyone, the response was a resounding yup. "There are certain symptoms germane to heartbroken women that you look out for," said one guy. Like what? we asked. "Bruises," one droll fellow replied. "Scars," said another. Besides those two funny, funny comics, though, there were some specific warning signs that seemed legit. About 25 percent of these guys listed skittishness and unpredictability at the top of their lists. "A woman on the rebound carries all kinds of emotional baggage, and she'll fly from one mood to the next," said one respondent. "Regular women are moody enough for me." Another popular beef among 40 percent of our men was the idea that they were merely filling a void. "She's got a boyfriend slot and she wants to drop me in it," said one man. Said another, "You end up cleaning up after her ex-boyfriend, fixing everything he broke on the way out." According to one guy, "You can end up talking to her for hours on end about her old relationship—it's too ego-shaking to hear about how great some other guy is." Others feared that the woman in question would be too distant, or too clingy, and a small fraction (5 percent) were afraid of being used. "I'm not saying that all women are manipulative," said one of the men we polled, "but say, for example, she's only dating me to make her old boyfriend jealous. I refuse to be some woman's pawn."

9. So do men avoid dating women on the rebound? Or do they ever actually seek them out?

Although no man openly admitted to seeking out vulnerable, rebounding women, about 50 percent confessed that they might take advantage of one if a fortuitous situation presented itself. "If some woman comes up to me in a bar and announces she's just broken up with some guy and she wants to sleep around for a while, you'd have to be a jerk to turn her down," said one. The other half, though, claimed you'd have to be a jerk to take the plunge. "It's a fool's game," said one of our abstainers. "She's not in a stable point of her life; if you cavalierly sleep with a heartbroken woman, you're just looking for trouble." One lone optimist said, "At least if she just broke up with someone, you know that she's had a boyfriend before, that she's capable of sustaining an intimate relationship with some-one." No one else echoed his sentiment, however. Our advice: You don't have to announce on your first date that you've just (been) jounced. Men like mystery—this is one thing you can keep to yourself.

10. Does he want or expect sex on the first date? How many dates will he wait? Is sex different with a woman who's just out of a long relationship? Will he think differently about me if I sleep with him on the first date?

"Do I want sex?" asked one respondent. "Of course I want it, but I don't expect to get it." That sentiment was echoed by just about every guy we polled. And whereas 20 percent of the guys said they'd wait as long as they had to for sex (some qualified that by saying they would wait indefinitely only if they were getting sex elsewhere during that time), most of them said they'd throw in the towel after three to five dates.

As for whether or not sex is weird with a heartbroken woman, that, of course, depends on the woman. Those of you who enjoy weird sex will, no doubt, continue the practice. From a guy's point of view, when it comes to the recently jilted, it isn't the sex, it's the stuff that happens around it that can get weird. "I started dating a woman four days out of a three-year relationship and the sex was amazing," said one. "Physically, we never had any problems—but emotionally, it was a minefield. In the first month, we talked about major commitment, moving in together, marriage—it was intense. Six weeks later she went back to her old boyfriend. No warning, no nothing—boom, she was gone." Another guy told us that his rebound woman was "incredibly shy. She must have been afraid of me. She wouldn't let me kiss her for two weeks. And then it took another two weeks just to get her bra off. It was over fifteen dates before I actually saw her naked." Give this guy points for being such a brave little trooper.

Finally, on the subject of having sex on the first date, there was no clear consensus. Thirty-five percent of our respondents said that they would think differently about a woman who did—and not in a favorable way. "A woman who jumped into the sack with me on Thursday might be doing it on Friday and Saturday with two other guys, for all I know," said one man. "That makes me wonder what kind of person she is." Fifty-five percent claimed it wouldn't change their opinion of the woman at all—but added that having sex early on would set a more casual tone to the relationship. And 5 percent said it depended on the sex—great sex would pique their interest, bad sex would turn them away. In other words, when it comes to sex and dating—and life, for that matter—your best tactic is just to go ahead and do what you want. Isn't that what you were going to do anyway?

9

Just When You Thought You Were Over Him . . .

PICTURE IF you will: It's early October. The smell of autumn is brisk and sharp in the air, breaking through the oppressive humidity of the last few weeks. You no longer arrive at work with your head all sweaty, looking like a used hankie. Your shoes have stopped sticking to the street. Thank god for fall—summer was the dregs. You're all over this cool weather.

And then.

Out of nowhere, the mercury shoots up. Indian summer. For one last weekend, you wear your cutoffs and sit in the sun. You begin to think longingly of lazy, lolling days on the beach. You forget how you used to lose half the skin on your thighs every time you tried to get out of your car. You forget about sticky, sleepless nights. Summer never looked so good. You love summer. Summer's the best. Why did it have to end?

No, you haven't accidentally opened the *Farmer's Almanac*. See, it's still us, Val and El. We're just getting a metaphor thing happening, to illustrate a point. That being: You can be buzzing through your life, feeling almost normal, hardly dwelling on your ex at all. And just when you think that you're finally over him, *wham*, something slams into you. Out of the blue, you're . . . blue. Without explanation, you miss him all over again, maybe even worse than you did before. It's so unexpected. It's so unusual. What horrible thing is happening to you now?

We like to call this knotty little phenomenon Indian heartbreak. Everyone experiences it, but few of us discuss it. Like menopause, we're oddly embarrassed by it. We think that this lapse is a sign of weakness. That it means we're maladjusted or something. That it's an indication that we've lost the only true love in our life and we'll never get over him.

Hardly. The bad news about Indian heartbreak is that it's no company picnic. The good news is, it's no company picnic. What's more, it's usually the last gulch to cross in the long obstacle course that is your breakup. Just as you need to hit the bottom of the pool in order to push up to the surface, your emotions need to take one more downward dip before they can start a steady climb upward.

So let's do what we do best and pick apart this feeling until it no longer resembles anything at all. Remember the upshot on this last heartbreak hurrah—after this, it's all downhill.

What It Is

Well, you have the general idea: Indian heartbreak is basically a second wind in your breakup depression. What makes it different from the first rush of tears? In a nutshell: time. You've had time to process what happened; you might even think you've recovered from it all quite nicely, thanks. And just when you think that you've stabilized, you find yourself singing a whole new set of sad songs. Which makes sense if you think about it. All the thrashing about you did in the immediate breakup aftermath was just to keep your head above water. It was about survival, not form or technique. Now that you know how to swim, you're faced with the struggle of finding out which stroke works best for you.

Which still leaves you waterlogged. Just because Indian heartbreak means that you're on the way to a healthy comeback doesn't mean it's any fun. Most of the women we talked to said that this second wave was less dramatic and hysterical than the first, but more despairing. "It was a mellow kind of depression," says one twenty-seven-year-old public relations exec. "I wasn't all riled up; I just felt like life sucked. I accepted that I was just one of those people who would never meet someone; I accepted that my life was a miserable, empty shell. I figured I would just resign myself to the facts instead of crying about them. I stopped talking about my ex. I stopped going on dates—I had gone on a million and hated them all. I was so picky—one guy had a freckle on his lip, and I hated him for that. It was pointless. Everything seemed pointless. I wasn't sad, I was bitter. I decided I didn't care if I was alone. I got into a routine of my own. My apartment was my best friend—I even felt sad to leave it in the morning."

Almost everyone seconded this experience. "I had this terrible sense of waiting for something good to happen," a twenty-nine-year-old TV programmer recalls. "It was like I was waiting for a voice-mail message that would change everything. When it didn't come, I was angry, resentful. I walked around as though there were a black cloud over my head; I couldn't shake it. It was a quiet time; I just wanted to be left alone. In a way, I was bitter because I felt pressured to get out there, but I just didn't want to. I felt guilty for my reclusiveness—and bitter because I didn't want to have to feel guilty." Another woman describes this period as "the time when my hate for one person—my ex—metamorphosed into hate for the whole world." And a thirty-one-year-old actress says she "experienced severe mood swings. I was surly, cranky as hell. Whereas right after the breakup I was morose and couldn't eat a thing, now I was aggressive. I said fuck it and ate everything in sight. I didn't hide my feelings. I stopped pretending to be happy for my girlfriends who were getting married or starting new relationships. On the whole, I was an incredibly unpleasant person."

According to Dr. Bonnie Eaker-Weil, a relationship therapist in New York City, Indian heartbreak is the final stage of soul-searching that has to occur before you can embark on another relationship. "At first," she says, "you might spend a lot of time doing things that help you avoid the pain—crying, railing against your ex-boyfriend, going out like crazy, holing up. Then, things even out a little. You start to date at a fairly steady pace; you might even be feeling pretty optimistic. But as time passes, you find yourself meeting more and more people whom you simply can't connect with, maybe people who are just as sad and lonely as you are. You realize afresh what you lost. You idealize your ex—and then won't give anyone else a chance because they naturally can't compare to the icon you've created in your head. This is generally when you distance yourself from the world and take time to think about yourself. You become extremely reflective about your breakup. Although you've mourned before, now you finally have the strength to step back and start the healing process. And while this is healthy, you have to be careful not to fall into it for too long. Being introspective and reflective is good, but you can't use it as an excuse to keep from rejoining life."

What Sets It Off

Oh, just about anything—depression never needs a formal invitation in order to come a-calling. For some women, Indian heartbreak is the perfect topper to a general feeling of malaise. "I think it was just the drudgery of dating that made me think that I missed him all over again," says one twenty-eight-year-old woman. Says another, "I looked at my life one day and it wasn't anything the way I thought it would be. I thought I'd have a glamorous job, a glittering social life, a handsome boyfriend, a great apartment. And there I was, busting my ass in a lousy job, eating frozen dinners in a cramped studio sublet, all alone. I went out on dates that left me completely cold. I was suddenly so disappointed, so malcontent. I blamed it on the fact that I didn't have a boyfriend. I started to believe that if I could have hung on to him, everything else that I wanted would have eventually come."

For other women, the triggering device is a little more specific, although no more logical. "It hit me when I was turning the clocks back for daylight savings time," a thirty-two-year-old doctor recalls. "I thought to myself, 'God, when we broke up, it was the day that we turned the clock forward. Has it been six months already?' It dawned on me that our separation was a reality. It was fact—it was no longer unusual or interesting. The breakup was old news—I no longer had the immediate emotion of it all to connect me to my ex. I wasn't mourning anymore—he was a thing of the past. I was totally unattached. I had never felt so alone."

A large number of women found that Indian heartbreak had the unnerving habit of settling in over holidays or birthdays. "I was sitting at my birthday party with a bunch of friends," says a twenty-six-year-old grad student, "and I looked around at all the smiling faces and thought, 'Where is he? Why isn't he here?' I burst into tears. I hadn't really been thinking about him for a while—we had been broken up for four months—but then it hit hard. I missed him for a long time after that. It wasn't a sharp pain, but more of a dull ache that stayed with me for about a month." And many counted weddings (not theirs) as major contributors to the misery index. "Two months after the breakup, I was a bridesmaid in an old friend's wedding," says a twenty-seven-year-old book publicist. "I had been helping her plan the wedding for about a year and a half; my ex had been there through it all. I stood there in my ugly bridesmaid dress and just couldn't believe that he wasn't there to laugh about it with me. I even looked for his face in the crowd; it was so inconceivable that I should be there without him. Then, an hour later, my best friend announced her engagement at the reception. It was too much for me. I was happy for my friends, but it just highlighted my own unhappiness even more. I felt completely hollow. It was a terrible night."

The majority of the women we spoke to, however, found that their Indian heartbreak was spurred on by a bad date or transition relationship. "My depression started the minute the new guy I had been dating walked out the door," says a twenty-six-year-old teacher. "I didn't care at all about him and I guess he could sense it. He broke it off, but I wasn't arguing. When he was gone, I sat in the living room, missing my old boyfriend like crazy. I thought, why me? Why do I have to be upset again? I knew then that I had blown it with the one person in the world that I was compatible with. I contemplated the next hundred years of solitude. And then I called my ex, for the first time in months. I knew it wasn't a good idea, but I couldn't help myself."

Oh, we could be all disapproving. We could make clucking noises and shake our heads.

VAL: I know exactly how she feels.

ELLEN: You can say that twice.

V: I know exactly how . . .

E: Oh, for god's sake, I'll go first. Two weeks after Jake and I broke up, I started dating a guy named Barney that I was sort of friends with. He was also out of a big relationship— he'd called off a wedding about four or five months earlier.

V: So both of you were members of the walking wounded.

E: In a way, yes, although I was probably in much earlier stages of convalescence than he was. Anyway, we went on a first date to the ballet and had a great time. For the next few months, we saw each other on and off—not in any regular way, just whenever the urge hit.

V: Ah yes, the urge . . .

E: We got along well and liked each other just fine, but there was no perceptible spark between us; there was definitely no love thing happening. We were totally incompatible— he was really obsessive about food and working out and watching his weight . . .

V: So not for you.

E: So not. And I think he thought I was a little too wild.

V: You? Little Miss Classical-Piano-and-Violin-Player? Little Miss Potpourri-in-the-Bathroom? Wild??

E: I know, I know. Which gives you some idea of his breathless spontaneity. At any rate, we liked each other the way we always had—as friends. Nothing more, nothing less. I think we slept together out of boredom more than incredible attraction.

V: And how was it?

E: Short. I mean, brief. I would say he was a remarkably concise lover. We did it only a couple of times. Neither of us could really be bothered.

V: Always a good sign. And then what?

E: And then nothing. My life was settling into a regular routine—work, friends, an occasional date. I felt like I was doing okay—I had gotten over the hurdle of the "first date" and sex with someone new with flying colors. Then, Barney and I went to see a play one night and had dinner, after which he came back to my apartment. Why, I don't know. We sat and stared at each other; he looked as bored as I felt, and he left after about ten minutes.

v: From the way you describe it, that would've been enough time to do it at least a dozen times.

e: Yeah, but we didn't even do it once. He just left; we gave each other a halfhearted good-night kiss. As I was closing the door, we kind of looked at each other ruefully, like, well so much for that—we tried and it didn't work. I remember standing in the middle of the room and thinking, "Can this really be my life? Everything I do is shit—totally pointless. Nothing means anything anymore." Even though the evening had been relatively benign—albeit somewhat of a snooze—I was left with a feeling of utter hopelessness. I called up my friend Howie . . .

v: . . . to the rescue . . .

e: . . . and when he said, "What's wrong?" I started sobbing. It was the first time I had really broken down, post-Jake. He said, "El, I don't understand; it's been months and you've been fine. So you had a not-great date—you don't even like the guy." And I just kept sobbing, "It's not that, I just hate this, I don't want it to be like this, I never thought it would be this way." I don't think he fully got it. He finally came over to my apartment and sat with me, sort of mute with sympathy, although the look on his face kind of said, "This girl is loco, get me out of here."

v: Poor Howie.

e: Forget poor Howie—poor *me*.

v: Yeah, well, obviously. If it makes you feel any better, I know the feeling.

E: I know you do.

V: Of course you do, you were there with me. So you remember how I started dating Joe a couple of months after the death of Mark?

E: All too well. That's how you and I became friends—you found out that Joe and I had gone to school together.

V: Right, I kept asking you to dig up information about him for me. I met him at a bar and we went out the night after. We were immediately attracted to each other. When we finally had sex . . .

E: . . . *finally*, like a whole day later . . .

V: . . . it was really out there. I liked the sex so much, I somehow managed to convince myself that I liked him, too. I threw myself into the relationship, if you can call it that. I bought sexy underwear, I depilitated like crazy, I was like a . . . like a . . .

E: Hairless woman possessed?

V: Close enough. I think maybe I needed him to like me, not because I thought he was so great, but because I wanted to feel desired. Like I was a hot property.

E: Which, of course, you are.

V: Thanks. Unfortunately, he didn't see it that way. He yanked me around like a yo-yo. He wouldn't call for days, and then he'd call out of the blue and want to screw. For some stupid reason, I always accommodated him. I let him treat me like a total—

E: Slut?

V: Close enough. I became something I never wanted to be— clingy, whiny, shrill. I practically screamed, "Pay attention to me! Pay attention to me!" He didn't. Finally, he just stopped calling. Finito. He didn't even have the decency to say that it was over. He just disappeared.

E: The cretin.

V: The thing is, I never really liked him so much as a person.

I just wanted some intimacy, however forced. I slept with him because I wanted to get close to him. But no matter how many times we did it, no matter how much time I spent with him, I wasn't satisfied; I just couldn't get him . . .

E: Close enough.

V: Exactly. When I realized that he wouldn't be knocking on my door ever again, I felt lost. I was hurt. I felt terrible about myself. And I missed Mark more than ever. It was easy for me to say, "Joe was a jerk; who needs him?"

E: Which you did, over and over.

V: But now that the distraction of having Joe was gone, I realized that Mark was the one who was still in my thoughts. Once again, I felt myself falling into a depression. It was weird, totally out of my control. I didn't know . . .

What to Do

V: I wasn't prepared for feeling this way, a second time around.

E: Who could be, really?

V: No one. I retreated from guys. I went for an emergency tune-up session with my shrink. And I spent the rest of my time hanging out with you.

E: Yup. You must've slept over at my house about three times a week for the next two months. Remember how we made crank calls in the middle of the night to Joe?

V: Sure. That was good for me—hanging out with a female friend, not feeling any pressure. In a way, I became a hermit, I removed myself from the world—with the extra, added bonus of having my pal El to cook me dinner.

E: Or order it out, anyway. That's kind of what I did—except my food deliverer was Howie.

V: Do tell.

E: Basically, after Barney, I decided to weld myself to Howie's side for the next month or so. I went everywhere with him. I turned down all offers to be set up—I didn't want to date—and lived my life for a while as Howie's charge. Of course everyone then tried to convince me that I should just go out with Howie . . .

v: . . . me included . . .

e: . . . but he and I knew better than that. It was perfect: I was up and around with a member of the male persuasion, so people stopped nagging me about dating. I never would have made it through that awful Indian heartbreak without him.

v: Nor I without you.

As opposed to plain old heartbreak, where reactions were all over the board, with Indian heartbreak, every one of the women we interviewed agreed that this was prime time for taking a hiatus from men. "I just didn't care about seeing anyone," says a twenty-seven-year-old market analyst. "I felt for the first time in my life that I was alone and loving it." "I took care of myself," says a twenty-five-year-old law student. "I worked and spent time with female friends—I went easy on myself." "I completely withdrew," says an entertainment lawyer. "I screened all my phone calls. I made plans by myself on the weekends. It made me feel confident and in control to have dinner for one. I felt like people would look at me and think how cool it was that I wasn't afraid to be by myself."

What else can you do? Dr. Eaker-Weil suggests that you take this time to resolve to move ahead and not look back. "Really, three times a day, try to think negatively about your ex," she says. "Train yourself to de-idolize him. On the other side, think positively about new people. When you try to compare the new with the old, make a conscious effort to stop yourself. Tell yourself that you're only sabotaging yourself by staying connected with an old life—one that didn't work for you anyway."

When It Breaks

Just as Indian heartbreak can arrive with little or no warning, so, too, can it leave. "I was just getting used to being in another blue funk, when it went away," says a thirty-two-year-old personnel director. "One morning, I woke up and I thought, 'Hey, I don't feel so bad.' I can't really think of any specific event that led up to this. I guess it just ran its course. I was sick and tired of feeling sick and tired—I was ready to meet new people again." Another woman remembers how "I snapped out of it in the middle of working out. I was in full swing, doing a step-aerobics class, when it suddenly popped into my head: 'I'm fine! I'm really doing okay. I have things to do; I can enjoy myself—I don't want to stay mired in the past, I like going on with my life.' It was weird; it was kind of like an epiphany or something. I don't know why it happened then. But the feeling of relief when I finally realized all this was unbelievable. I felt a hundred pounds lighter. I felt like going out and celebrating—so I did."

And then there are the women who can pinpoint exactly how their second wave of depression passed. "For a long time, when I got in bed, I used to imagine that I could turn back time and go back to the way it used to be, when my ex and I were living together," remembers a twenty-seven-year-old newspaper reporter. "You know that movie, *Somewhere in Time*, where Christopher Reeve goes back to get Jane Seymour? That's what I used to think about. One night, I had a dream that I actually did it. There was my old boyfriend in our old apartment, telling me he loved me, asking me to take him back. And instead of feeling ecstatic, I was horrified. I realized, 'I don't love him anymore. I thought I wanted this, but I don't. I've made a terrible mistake.' I prayed that I could change things back again. When I woke up, I was so happy. Not long after that, I started dating again and met the person I'm with today."

Another woman recalls how she reached her letting-go point when "I saw an announcement in the paper that my ex had gotten married. It was as if a door finally swung shut in my brain. I thought, 'That's it, there's no going back now, even if you want to. Pining over him would be a waste of time—and haven't I wasted enough time already?' It was such a practical end to such an emotional time—but I guess I was finally ready to let go. The wedding announcement just gave me the final nudge in the right direction."

Finally, there's the large contingent who say that they could get past Indian heartbreak only when they met another man. Maybe, maybe not. "You might think you've finally recovered because you met a great guy and are starting up a new relationship," says Dr. Eaker-Weil, "but you have to remember that the reason you met him was because you were ready to. A man can't magically chase the blues away. You have to do that first. When you do, then you're equipped to share yourself with someone with whom you can build something good and lasting."

We agree completely. You can't hail a cab unless you're strong enough to lift your arm first (or you can do that thing where you stick two fingers in your mouth and make one of those really loud, piercing whistles). And if you've made it this far, odds are you'll be strong enough to hail a whole fleet of cabs, if you're so inclined. Maybe even strong enough to hear the harebrained thing we're going to say next without falling down, beating your fists on the floor, and screaming, *"Lies, all lies!"*

So here goes. After all these pages of kvetching about the

guys in our lives, after all the ruckus about those crazy, mixed-up men, after the reams and reams of we're so super/they're so stupid, we've got to say this one thing: Men, by and large, are a pretty terrific invention. Come on. Admit it. Even the women we spoke to who were in the throes of heartbreak despair could drag up at least one or two good things about the male of the species. And we're not only referring to men as boyfriends or dates or sex toys (although they, too, have a definite draw)—we're talking in broader terms. We're talking about the guy on the airplane who helps you stuff your suitcase in the overhead luggage compartment, or the man in the deli who always saves you the last onion bagel, or your doorman who gives you a big welcome-home smile after you come back from vacation. So we thought it was only fair to offer up at least . . .

Five Reasons to Love Men

1. Because they put up with us. Face it: What seems like perfectly normal behavior to us is bona fide alien-nation stuff to them. And yet, often, with great grace and good humor, men do their level best to accommodate the needs of these strange female creatures. One woman recalls how a guy she befriended in an Austrian airport walked all over said airport with her in a feverish, furious quest to purchase . . . a lipstick. "I had lost my luggage and I felt so grungy and unkempt," she says. "I just really needed some lipstick. This guy, Jan, walked from kiosk to kiosk with me for about an hour. He really tried to be helpful—he kept holding up mascaras and sunblocks and saying, 'Is this what you're looking for?' The only time he got irritable was when we finally found some and the shop-keeper accidentally tried to sell me the wrong color. Jan acted as though the guy had tried to kill my whole family or something—he was so indignant and adamant that I get exactly what I want."

Another woman remembers how she and a male co-worker used to go every day to pick up lunch at a deli nearby. "I was on a diet at the time. I used to order the same salad—just lettuce and tomato, no avocado, no croutons, and just vinegar, no oil, on the side. I made a real stink about it; I must have seemed like such a little fusspot—like Sally from *When Harry Met Sally*. Very high-maintenance. Anyway, one day, we got back to the office and Chip unpacked the bag. He looked at my salad and exploded, 'Those idiots! They didn't put your dressing on the side! And there are croutons all over the place! How the hell do they expect you to eat this?' Before I could stop him, he had stormed out, salad in hand, determined to right this great wrong that had been done to me. I loved him for that. Because it was important to me, it became important to him."

Basically, even if it doesn't make sense to them, men will, more often than not, do their best to keep their mouths shut and go along with the whole rigmarole. They can be a pretty accepting bunch—which is more than we can say for us. So the next time you're tempted to snatch the remote control out of the hands of your brother or roommate (or even your new boyfriend?) and shake it in his face and scream, "*What is this, an extension of your penis?*" stop and think about the night he unquestioningly walked around with an extra pair of black stockings in his breast pocket, in case the ones you were wearing sprouted a run. And then shake it in his face anyway. You can't help yourself.

2. Because they don't want us to be afraid. Sure, we're brave and independent. We are woman, hear us roar. But there are still times when even the most self-sufficient of us can turn into shrinking violets. When we might feel paralyzed with fear. Times when it can be awful nice to turn to some guy and silently mouth, "Help!"

Which is, more often than not, exactly what he'll do. At the top of the list of Situations Where We'd Most Like to Have a Man Around the House are those that involve visitors from the insect world. "For three years, I would call my super to come up and kill waterbugs in my bathroom," said a thirty-year-old New York district attorney. "They were so big; they terrified me. Every time he came up, he'd give me an indulgent smile and then quickly whisk the thing down the toilet. When I apologized profusely, he'd always say, 'No, no, I understand; they're big, these waterbugs. Hard to kill.' He never made me feel ridiculous or wimpy. And he never complained about doing it." Another New Yorker told us how she used to tape paper cups upside-down over roaches she found in her kitchen and then have a male friend who lived a block away come over and dispose of them. "I couldn't stand the crunching noise they made when I stepped on them," she says. "It was scary enough just trapping them under the cups. I needed my friend to do the rest. He was always nice about it—he'd try to make me feel better by telling me that it wasn't a roach, it was a piece of food, or a ball of lint, or a paint chip. Once he even tried to tell me it was a ladybug. He wanted me to think that I didn't have a roach problem; he didn't want me to stress out about it."

But bug squashing isn't the only way that guys can soothe our fears. Don't forget all the times a guy has insisted on driving or walking you home after dark, the way he'll wait in the car until he sees that you're safely in the door. A woman who felt nervous about living in a first-floor apartment regularly depended on the kindness of neighbors—more specifically, her upstairs neighbor. "We had become good friends, and often we'd go out at night, to dinner or a movie," she says.

"When we got back, if it was late, I would be anxious about walking into a dark apartment. It was irrational—the building was perfectly safe—but I was always afraid that someone would be lurking in the shadows somewhere. We fell into a routine—I'd unlock the door and he'd say, 'Wait here,' and then he'd go methodically from room to room, switching on lights and looking into closets. Then he'd say, 'All safe,' and I'd go in. It was so silly—I knew it and he knew it—but he always acted as though my fears were perfectly normal and legitimate. He never made me feel stupid about it."

Or what about the woman who was watching a video with a good male friend when a rather spectacular car accident occurred, right outside her window. "We heard the screeching of tires and then the crunch of metal. He looked out the window, gasped, and then, right away, turned to me and said, 'Don't look. Don't look—you'll be scared.' Then he ran to call 911. Of course I eventually looked anyway—some poor motorcyclist was lying on the street under a car—but I always remember how my friend's first thought was to save me the awful sight. In that totally inappropriate moment, I felt happy that he was such a good friend to me."

3. Because they hurt when we hurt. When something bad happens in our lives, our female friends are always good for commiseration and advice. "That stinks," they'll nod sympathetically. Or, "You should just march in there and give her a piece of your mind," they'll say indignantly. When you tell a guy about the latest trauma in your life, he might not be so adept with the hand-holding and the counseling. But most of the women we talked to agreed that men, more than women, feel other people's pain. Where they're lacking in sympathy, they usually make up for in empathy.

They're a loyal bunch, these men. When you come home shaken by a nasty episode at work, he gets personally pissed off for you. You can see it in the way his jaw tightens or how he walks around in circles and hits the wall. When someone does you wrong, they've done him wrong, too. "A co-worker once stabbed me in the back and I told a guy friend of mine about it," a thirty-five-year-old movie agent says. "He was livid. It was as if he were the one who had been betrayed. All my girlfriends had been nice about it, but he was actually hurt. He obsessed over it; he kept bringing it up for weeks afterward. In the end, things got straightened out in the office, but to this day, he still hates that co-worker. He begrudges her my pain almost more than I do."

Another woman tells of how she once went on a date that ended up bordering on rape. "When I relayed the story to my female friends," she says, "they were appropriately shocked and outraged. And then we'd start talking about something else. But when I told my male friends about it, the universal sentiment was 'I'd like to kill that guy.' They couldn't get past it. Every one of them wanted to seek revenge — for me. The idea that my physical well-being was in danger infuriated them beyond the bounds of normal friendship. And even though it was a horrible experience, it also made me see how many good guys there are — and how lucky I was to have them on my side."

4. Because they shoulder so many burdens on their own. We women pretty much subscribe to a share-and-share-alike life philosophy. Whether we've won or lost, we're quick to let everyone know the score. Women are famous for their support systems, their coffee klatches, their emotional networks. And experts pretty much agree that it's the psychologically healthy way to go.

But all this confabulation doesn't come quite as easily to men. "When my best guy friend's grandmother died, he didn't tell anyone for three days," says one twenty-five-year-old woman. "He walked around looking pained and bewildered but never said a word. When he finally told me the news, I said, 'Why didn't you say anything sooner?' He said, 'I needed to have it for myself. I needed to sort through it first.' My heart ached for him—I wished that I could make everything all better, that he could look to me for strength instead of bearing it all alone."

Men are taught early on to hide their feelings. They're usually pretty good at it. But every now and then, you catch glimpses: You see them silently registering defeat, speeding off in cars or walking angrily down streets, cursing and brushing away demons that only they can see. They may travel in loud, raucous groups, swinging bravado, but at the end of the day, so much more than us women, they go it alone.

Perhaps men and women need each other equally. But women can express that need more easily. Because of this, as much as we would welcome their heads on our shoulders, more often than not it's our heads that are doing the leaning. More often than not men will, in their own sweet, clumsy way, do their level best to show us that the world can be a friendly place.

5. Because they see the good over the bad. Oh, we can be a critical breed, we women. The wrong color socks can send us over the edge. We notice anything and everything— particularly things that we perceive as bad or ugly or stupid. We sweat the details. We give very little leeway: "Oh, sure, her hair is okay, but she has such a square jaw. And her hips are so lumpy. And did you get a look at those boots?" When we're with a guy—be it a boyfriend or a brother or a friend— the critical meter goes into overdrive. We—well yes, we nag a little. "Don't shovel your food into your mouth," we'll say. "Stop shuffling around like that, stand up straight. Don't breathe through your nose."

Men, on the other hand, have an endearing way of . . . skipping over the bad parts. "You don't have a big butt," one might say to you. "It's curvy. It's sexy. I think it's great." What's more, they really mean it—since men don't know from etiquette, you can pretty much count on their sincerity. "A friend of mine used to listen to me and my girlfriends complain about all manner of cosmetic ills," says a twenty-eight-year-old writer. "We'd bemoan this or that—crooked teeth, a scar, a cowlick, laugh lines. And every time, he'd shake his head and say, 'You're crazy. It gives you character.' We would laugh him off, but it still made us feel good to know that he could see something nice in what we perceived as terrible flaws."

In other words, men don't go searching for the blots and stains that we so eagerly seek out. When they look at us, they instinctively see us as the good, whole, desirable people that they really believe we are. And by and large, they treat us accordingly. So even if you do hit upon the occasional bad apple in the bunch, once you get your bearings, you'll find that there are still bushels of men who are willing to show you how wonderful you are. Let them.

And then don't forget to return the favor.

songs and movies to recover by

You've sung all the sad songs you can stand by this point in your breakup evolution. We say, no more tears on your pillow. No more pain in your heart. Thought there was just no getting over him? Guess again—you will survive. You'll have a better love next time around. Sing loud, sing proud. There's a new day a-dawning. Mourning has broken.

"Alive and Kicking" — Simple Minds

"All Cried Out" — Lisa Lisa and Cult Jam

"All She Wants to Do Is Dance" — Don Henley

"Another One Bites the Dust" — Queen

"Back on My Feet Again" — Babies

"The Bitch Is Back" — Elton John

"Born to Run" — Bruce Springsteen

"Brand New Me" — Dusty Springfield

"Breakin' In a Brand New Heart" — Connie Francis

"Don't Call Us, We'll Call You" — Sugarloaf

"Don't Come Around Here No More" — Tom Petty

"Don't Worry, Be Happy" — Bobby McFerrin

"Feeling Alright" — Joe Cocker

"Feelin' Groovy" — Simon and Garfunkel

"Finally Got Myself Together" — Impressions

"Fortress Around Your Heart" — Sting

"Free Bird" — Lynyrd Skynyrd

"Freedom" — Wham!

"Go Your Own Way" — Fleetwood Mac

"Gonna Get Along Without You Now" — Patience and
Prudence

"Haven't Got Time for the Pain" — Carly Simon

"Heart Like a Wheel" — Steve Miller Band

"Hold Your Head Up" — Argent

"I Am a Rock" — Simon and Garfunkel

"I Will Survive" — Gloria Gaynor

"I'm Free" — Who

"I'm Looking for a New Love, Baby" — Jodi Watley

"I'm Still Standing" — Elton John

"It Doesn't Matter Anymore" — Buddy Holly

"The Last Worthless Evening You'll Ever Spend" — Don Henley

"Live for Today" — Grass Roots

"No Looking Back" — Michael McDonald

"No More Tears (Enough Is Enough)" — Donna Summer and
Barbra Streisand

"One Fine Day" — Carole King

"Over You" — Gary Puckett
"Que Sera, Sera" — Doris Day
"Respect" — Aretha Franklin
"Respect Yourself" — Staple Sisters
"Sisters Are Doin' It for Themselves" — Eurythmics and Aretha Franklin
"Stand!" — Sly and the Family Stone
"Stayin' Alive" — Bee Gees
"That's It, I Quit, I'm Moving On" — Sam Cooke
"These Boots Are Made for Walking" — Nancy Sinatra
"Turn, Turn, Turn" — Byrds
"We're Not Gonna Take It" — Twisted Sister
"You Ain't Seen Nothing Yet" — Bachman-Turner Overdrive

GIRL GETS BOY

The Big Easy
Bull Durham
Choose Me
Crossing Delancey
Moonstruck
An Officer and a Gentleman
Prelude to a Kiss
Pretty in Pink
Say Anything
Sixteen Candles
Sleepless in Seattle
When Harry Met Sally
Working Girl

UNLIKELY LOVE FOUND

Big
Continental Divide
Defending Your Life
Desperately Seeking Susan

Earth Girls Are Easy
Making Mr. Right
Splash
Tootsie

AND IF YOU CAN BELIEVE THIS . . .

Dances with Wolves
Harold and Maude
Pretty Woman
The Princess Bride
Risky Business
White Palace

STILL WANT TO SEE HIM SUFFER?

Heartburn

10

The Beginning of the Beginning

ALL GOOD things have to start somewhere. There was the first nervous day of that new job you never thought you'd get, the first day you brought little Theo home from the ASPCA, the first day you woke up in a brand-new apartment. And then there was the first day you woke up in your by-then old apartment—in love with a brand-new guy. That's the day we're talking about.

We can hear your heart fluttering with fear. It's only natural. Opening yourself up to a new love can be an exercise in terror and exhilaration. Frankly, though, we've had enough of the terror stuff (if you haven't, chapter 5 is a particularly good refresher); we're ready to move on to the exhilaration portion of our program. Onward and upward: As someone once said (we think it was George Bush, but maybe it was Marvin Gaye), let's get it on.

So you wake up and he's still sleeping. You nudge him gently under the covers. He sighs, his eyelids flicker and he moans softly and rolls over, embracing you with his strong, muscular arm, tenderly pulling you closer, and closer still, until . . .

You're interrupted by our loud gagging noises. Sorry. To tell you the truth, despite the cornball nature of the above scenario, we've got to admit it doesn't sound too horrible. In fact, it sounds kind of good. In fact, if you overlook the morning breath and factor in the big honking early-A.M. hard-on, it's pretty much what we live for. You?

We thought so.

But what about when he leaves after breakfast, giving you a pat on the rear, a kiss on the forehead, and the promise that he'll call you . . . soon. And you're left wondering, *soon? Soon?* What the hell does *soon* mean? Two hours? Two days? Two weeks?

Steady, girl. Breathe deeply for two minutes. Before you churn yourself into butter, try to relax a little. This isn't your old relationship, that blasted heath, the source of so much pain. This is something new. This is the start of something good. *This is supposed to be the fun part.*

You don't believe us? We don't blame you. When it comes to that weird feeling in the cockles of your heart, no one can really deal—our emotionally stunted selves included. Sure, you might say that falling in love is like quitting smoking: It's easy; I've done it a thousand times. Still, no matter how many times you've taken the fall, it's only natural to feel a little jumpy from the get-go. Hey, you're wary. You don't want to spin out of control. You try to convince yourself that he doesn't really matter to you. He doesn't. Really. You might even be tempted to conjure up a mental checklist of really good reasons not to fall in love. Which, we feel obliged to point out, is just plain silly and counterproductive. Over-analytical and neurotic. In short, just our cup of tea.

A Mental Checklist of Really Good Reasons Not to Fall in Love

- It's too time-consuming. Hey, we're *busy*. There aren't enough hours in the day for all the working/phone-talking/clothes-trying-on that we have to do. We need roller skates to keep up with us. The last thing we want is to get all sidetracked by some boy with distracting, well-traveled hands that tangle your hair or untangle your limbs — and, by doing so, effectively kill an entire afternoon. Sometimes, the thought of how he does what he does can cause you to stare, dazed, at your computer screen for hours, until you slip into a trance. When you come to, you're furiously typing out reams of flowery prose that tell him, in some ridiculously roundabout way, how much you love . . . his hands. Please. Who has time for such nonsense?

- Being with someone for long periods of time can be a real snooze. Men can be a boring lot. They talk about sports. They talk about politics. They talk about movies about sports and politics. Every now and then, if you're really lucky (read: they want to sleep with you), they'll talk about themselves. Why bother shaving your legs just to listen to some guy drone on, when you can sit at home and have an ever so much more interesting conversation with your stubble?

Wait a minute, you might venture in protest, every now and then a girl happens upon a guy who's easy on the mind. Who can coax a smile out of her even when she's so mad she could spit. Who can make life open up a little wider, give her a little more to imagine, a little more to warm her heart. A boy whom she could happily stare at across the dinner table, chin in hands, straight through 'til morning.

Right. The next thing you're going to tell us is that you've met one.

- You haven't got room for the pain. It's one thing to meet a guy who just wants to toss a few into you. It's another thing entirely to get attached to him. Attached means that his trials spill into your life, that his tribulations become yours. That the occasional indigo of his moods will certainly, ever so slightly, tint yours. True, in exchange, he'll help you bear your burdens. And when the going gets tough, he'll make it less tough to get going. It's kind of tempting, but . . . nah. You've got enough to worry about already.

- You can't stand all that attention. You probably think that guys only look at stuff like cars and planes and breasts. You're partially right. But if a boy likes you, he'll cut into his car/plane/breast time to stare at . . . you. If you're in the same metropolitan area, he'll know where you are every minute. He's watchful: He quietly moves about, doing whatever he can to make you comfortable. He says things like "What do *you* want to do?" And in the meantime, you can barely concentrate for the loudness of his watching. You're scared you're going to do something to let him down. You're scared you're getting used to it.

Or maybe you're just plumb scared. The fact is, neither sleet nor snow nor dark of night nor dumb mental checklists can stay love's courier from its appointed rounds. And even though you vowed to yourself *never again*, the fact is, if you're already at the checklist stage, vows like that are about as sturdy as tumbleweed on toast. Face it, sister: You're gone. The best thing you can do at this point is go gladly and graciously.

Which is what all the women in this chapter did. Eventually. Of course, there was some preliminary agonizing — monsters under the bed and ghosts in the mind that had to be shooed away. But in all of the following stories (informally organized, as usual, for your reading pleasure), each woman slowly, surely went with her heart. Which, when it comes to great beginnings, is the only way to fly.

Hate at First Sight

Romantic chemistry is a weird science. Sometimes you can meet a guy and he'll conjure up fireworks and Tchaikovsky-inspired violins. Other times, it's more like firearms and Dosto-evsky-inspired violence. Like everything else in life, it can go either way.

As usual, we'll take the low road. A majority of the women we spoke to found that hate at first sight was far more common than its goopy love counterpart. Well, maybe *hate* is an overstatement, but disinterest, certainly. Distaste. Dislike. Dis.

When Courtney, a thirty-year-old art production coordinator, started her new job, "I was put in an office that I was sharing with some guy named David. He wasn't there at the time, because he never got into work before 4 P.M. Whenever I told anyone who my office-mate was, they'd laugh. And then they'd say something like 'Well, you're in for a treat.' I didn't know what to think.

"That day, I got a big bouquet of flowers from my old co-workers; my desk was so small there was no place to put it so, I put it on his desk. He wasn't there anyway. At four o'clock, David strolled in. He looked like he had just rolled out of bed, scruffy and surly. Not a real looker. He acted like a pompous jerk and made a big deal of moving the flowers back to my desk—he was incredibly obnoxious about it, muttering about how much space I had and how come I had to clutter up his desk.

"The next day, the flowers were in my way again, so I

moved them onto his desk. That afternoon, he moved them back. And it went back and forth that way, until three days later, I found them in the trash. I knew at that point that I was dealing with a Grade A Asshole.

"It took about six months of us grunting at each other before we actually started to have real conversations. He was smart, and when he wasn't being so cranky he could really make me laugh. After a while, we got into the groove of sharing an office; I realized that his crankiness was kind of a front for his shyness. We started hanging out together occasionally, going to concerts and movies. On his birthday, a bunch of us went out to dinner; afterward, he gave me a kiss on the cheek and I got all flustered. I don't know why—it was perfectly innocent—but my knees practically buckled.

"After that, we became fast friends; we went out together all the time. We gossiped together, told each other about bad dates we had gone out on, laughed about them. He told me that he only liked older women (I'm twelve years younger than him); I told him I liked blonds (he has dark hair). Then one day, he told me he'd met a cute younger woman that he liked. Suddenly I felt a huge rush of jealousy; I was green, through and through. That's when I realized how much I liked him.

"Nothing happened with the younger woman, thank god. A couple weeks later, we went to a concert together. We were standing in the audience and he put his arm around me. I got really nervous and was uncomfortable with the way I was leaning on him, but I didn't want to move. I didn't want him to know how aware I was that he was touching me. And I definitely didn't want him to take his arm away. I was frozen to the spot.

"The next night, we had plans to see a band and I decided to ask David if he wanted to come to my house for dinner before the show. He said, 'Fine, can I bring my friend Willa?' That hurt. Willa, it turns out, was a totally platonic friend—

a lesbian, in fact. We all had a great time. After the show, he walked me home. I was getting tired and depressed—he hadn't touched me once the whole night. I was discouraged. At the door, I asked him if he wanted to come up and watch television. He thought about it and said okay. We sat on the couch, and finally he turned to me and said, 'Should we keep this clean, or what?' I said, 'No!' and I kissed him. He looked a little startled, but not too startled to kiss me back. Now, we live together—and even though we don't share an office anymore, we share a bathroom.''

As Courtney found out, the power of hate at first sight should never be underestimated—after all, some believe that hate is only love that's lost its way. It's a possibility. In any case, for Gina, a twenty-nine-year-old grad student from Chicago, there were even greater odds than plain old enmity to overcome. Once again, however, hate-at-first-sight turned into a kinder, stronger feeling, just when she least expected it.

"I was engaged to a guy whose family were old friends with my family," she says. "We were at different graduate schools and planned to be married the next year. It was sort of picture-perfect: We had grown up together, been old childhood friends, high school sweethearts, and now we were going to be husband and wife. I certainly wasn't looking to date any-one.

"Midway into the semester, I went to a party, where there was this guy who stared at me the whole night. He never said a word to me—just stared and stared. He gave me the creeps. I found out his name was Charles, and then I spent the rest of the party trying, unsuccessfully, to stay out of his eyeshot.

"The next day, a guy friend of mine called and said, 'Charles really liked you. He wants to have dinner with you.' Then he asked if I wanted to go on a double date—him and his girlfriend, me and Charles. Well, I thought it was pretty ridiculous that Charles should like me; after all, we never even spoke. It was even more ridiculous that he had to get his friend to call me. I said, 'If he wants to ask me out, he can damn well call himself.' I figured that would nip it in the bud.

"Ten minutes later, the phone rang. It was Charles. I thought to myself, 'What a loser,' but as he stammered on and on, I decided, what the hell, I had no plans that weekend. Besides, it would be entertaining to watch him bumble around the whole evening. I could amuse myself with him. After about ten more minutes of conversation in which I was incredibly arch and sarcastic, I agreed to go. I laughed with my girlfriends over the fact that he would still want me to, after I had given him such a hard time.

"The night of the date rolled around, and I found myself facing Charles across a dinner table. I was all prepared to toy with him, to be the ultimate bitch-goddess, but I hadn't counted on one thing: He was no bumbler. He was smart and ambitious and kind. I was totally wrong about him. I was utterly taken aback, and I felt so guilty about being such a witch that I was practically silent the whole night. He kept looking at me quizzically but not saying anything.

"He walked me home and asked if everything was okay. I was so filled with remorse at this point that something came over me and I just blurted out, 'I'm so sorry, it's just that I feel like such a terrible person—I thought you were this total idiot, and meanwhile I'm the total idiot.' I was babbling; he looked confused. Finally, after a minute or so more of me spouting uselessly, he laughed and said, 'Do you always do this on the first date?' I said, 'Never.' He said, 'Do you want to try for a second date?' At which point I muttered, 'You know, I'm engaged,' and he said, 'I know. We'll go just as friends.' Which is exactly what we did for the next few months. We studied together, ate meals together, went to movies together, 'just as friends.' I became incredibly attached to him.

"Over winter break, I went home to New York and spent the month with my fiancé. Suddenly everything seemed so lackluster. I wasn't happy with him; all I could think about was Charles. I knew I had to do something. At the end of the vacation, I gave back my ring. I couldn't really give a reason—it wasn't like there was someone else, but then again, there was.

"I flew back to Chicago, and Charles was waiting for me at the airport. When I saw his face, I knew what I wanted to do. I threw my arms around him and said really fast—before I could think about how stupid I'd sound—'I love you. I want to be with you.' He didn't even miss a beat. He said right back, 'I love you, too. Welcome home.' Then I showed him my finger, minus the ring. A year later, there was another ring on it—this time from the right guy."

Romancing the Stone

Then there are the instances where you meet a guy and fall for him, hard, but there's one teensy problem: He doesn't fall back. We're talking unrequited love here. And while sometimes all the wooing and voodoo spells in the world won't melt his hard heart, at other times true love conquers all.

Take, for example, Emma, a twenty-eight-year-old retailer. "I met Joel over the summer, out in the Hamptons. My first reaction was god, he's cute. He said he thought the same. And even though it wasn't exactly love at first sight, there was a definite affinity. We were together a lot, in groups. We were both dating around at the time—no one serious—but I don't think either of us really thought of the other as a romantic possibility. It was too obvious or something.

"The problem was, the affinity eventually developed into a full-blown crush. For me, at least. He continued to show no signs of interest. I stopped dating; I was too preoccupied with Joel, or maybe just my fantasies of Joel. One night, toward the end of the summer, we were talking and he asked if I had seen the new Jackie Mason play. I had, but he hadn't. I knew a way to get free tickets, so I suggested that we go, and he said great, let's do it. I was so excited—I went to the guy in my office who got press tickets, but he told me that he didn't have them anymore. Then the show closed. I had been foiled.

"Then one morning I was walking by Radio City Music Hall, and I noticed that there was a Joe Jackson concert coming. I thought Joel might be into it. I asked the guy in my office if he could get tickets, but he couldn't. I decided to ask Joel if he wanted to go, then buy the tickets myself and pretend I had gotten them free, so he wouldn't think I was fawning over him.

"Next there was the problem of finding him—I knew he lived in Manhattan, but I didn't know his address or phone number. He was unlisted. I called around to all our mutual friends and finally got his number. By then, I was cutting it close for buying tickets, so although I had originally wanted to call him casually at the office; now I had to call him at home. I bit the bullet and dialed the phone. When he answered, I said, 'Hi, it's Emma, from the Hamptons. I couldn't get Jackie Mason, but I got Joe Jackson tickets. Do you want to go?' He waffled. I immediately said, 'If you don't want to, it's fine, blah, blah, blah,' but then he said he did. I hung up, called Radio City, and miraculously got the last two tickets they had. For fifty bucks apiece.

"We went to the concert, and nothing happened. He wasn't feeling well. We hardly talked about anything. I called him a couple times after the concert—I left messages on his machine—and he never called me back. I tried to hang out in the neighborhood where he worked, hoping I would bump into him. Once I actually did, and he was friendly but brief. I was beginning to feel pathetic, like I was hopelessly chasing him. I tried to forget him, but I couldn't. Then, one weekend, there was a reunion party for our house in the Hamptons. I prayed that he would be there; when he showed up, I thought I would die. We hung out together, drinking, flirting, and all of a sudden we realized that almost everyone was gone. We started making out—it was total heat. He took me home and asked me out for that Friday.

"He picked me up on Friday at my apartment. We sat down and started talking. Before we knew it, it was ten, and we realized we hadn't eaten. We ordered in. He stayed the night. That was two years ago—now we're engaged. When I think back on it, I was so silly, pursuing him like my life depended on it, lying about those Joe Jackson tickets. But it turns out that it was the best hundred dollars I ever spent."

For Emma, just getting the guy within chasing range was half the battle. For Claire, a twenty-seven-year-old market researcher, Mr. Right's proximity was no problem—he was her roommate. The tricky part was winning him over.

"Dylan and his friend Jim had taken an apartment with another guy," says Claire. "At the last minute, the third guy bailed. They put out an ad with a roommate finders' service, and I answered it. We all met at the apartment one Saturday. I liked it, they liked me, and the next month I moved in.

"Jim was practically married; he spent all his time with his girlfriend. But Dylan was single—with a vengeance. He went out every night, dancing, drinking, carousing. He had so much energy; he made everything fun and interesting. Plus, he was adorable and unbelievably smart. Girls loved him—me included.

"I remember the first time I saw him come out of the shower with just a towel on. I thought, my god, he's so beautiful. He was always nice to me, but he treated me more like a best friend or a sister. Even though I dated, Dylan was always it for me. I would sit in my room miserably and listen to him bring girls home; I'd actually hear them have sex. It was awful.

"One night, we went out to a party and got a little drunk. When we got home, we lay, comatose, in front of the TV. And then, I don't know what happened, we started fooling around. We slept together that night, and I was ecstatic. He wasn't, though. The day after, he said to me, 'That was a mistake; we shouldn't do that again. I don't want to ruin our friendship.' I pretended I agreed, but I was crushed.

"For a whole year following, we slept together maybe another four or five times. Every time we did it, we would say afterward that it was a big mistake. He dated like crazy—he'd fall in love every month. And then, when things didn't work out for him, he'd be back to old Claire, Claire who would always take care of him, ladling out sympathy and advice—and every now and then sex. It wasn't like he was taking advantage of me or anything—he was totally on the up and up—but what he didn't know was that I was completely stuck on him. I never admitted it, but as more and more time passed, I felt more desperate, more furious, every time he came home with some woman.

"We started to fight. In my frustration, I would start battles with him. I was a total shrew. Finally, after fifteen or twenty huge blowups, he shouted, 'What is the matter with you? What has come over you? Why are you like this?' I burst into tears and ran into my room, sobbing, 'You don't appreciate me; you only use me and meanwhile, I lu-huh-huh-huh-ve you.' I could barely get it out for all the crying I was doing. He said, 'Oh no. Oh god. What a mess,' and left the apartment.

"When he came back, he explained that he wasn't ready for a relationship. That it wasn't a good time in his life to have a steady girlfriend. That even though he cared for me, he didn't care for me that way. It was brutal. I felt beaten, humiliated. I made plans to move out in six weeks. He said he wished I didn't feel like I had to go, but that he understood.

"Moving day came, and I was finishing packing up my boxes. He was standing in the room watching me. I felt like I was moving underwater, my limbs were so heavy and sluggish. I didn't even want to look at him, I hurt so much. He kept trying to start a conversation with me, but I couldn't respond. Finally, after about an hour of practically uninterrupted silence, I looked up at him. His eyes filled with tears. He said, 'Please don't go—I was wrong. I love you so much.' We went into his bedroom—mine was all packed up, remember—and stayed there for the rest of the weekend. And even though it was a major pain to unpack everything all over again, with him there to help me, it didn't seem so bad."

Fear of Trying

So far, we've seen the women who run down men, and the women who run after men. What about the women who run away? It's a common reaction: "Love meant terror, plain and simple," says Ruth, a twenty-nine-year-old real estate agent. "I was hurt so badly, and after months of dating total losers after the breakup, I'd grown comfortable with the idea that I would never be in a relationship. I didn't want one—I was scared I'd make all the same stupid mistakes and get hurt again. My friends called me a wimp; they didn't understand why I was in avoidance mode. But I knew that I certainly wasn't going to throw myself in front of a moving train again."

And then she met Jack. "I'd met him before—we had mutual friends—and I'd always thought he was cute. One weekend, we met at a party; we talked for about an hour. That Monday, a friend of mine called me and said, 'Jack thought you were great. He wants to ask you out—what do you think?' I said sure and waited for him to call.

"Weeks went by and he didn't call. In the beginning I wondered why, but after a while I was glad he didn't. Then, three months later, out of the blue, he phoned me and asked me out. We made plans, but I was sure they would amount to nothing. To my surprise, we had a really good time. I actually liked him. But I kept telling myself that I didn't, that he would turn out to be just like all my other old boyfriends, another jerk. He didn't call the next day, anyway. Good riddance, I thought.

"A week later, he called—he had unexpectedly gone out of town for work—and asked me on another date. My first thought was that he was toying with me like a cat with a mouse, building me up for another painful fall. I almost canceled but then ended up going. And going and going. After about five dates, I heard myself say out loud to my best friend that I liked him. It was the last thing I expected, to care for him. Then I cried all night long. From then on, I didn't talk about the relationship with anyone for fear of jinxing it. Inside, though, I was a wreck. Now that I couldn't deny my emotions—to myself, at least—I was even more afraid. Out of pure fear, I ended up postponing a lot of our plans. Things went very slowly—every time I was able to take a step forward, I ran two steps back.

"He never betrayed me, though. He was always loving and patient with me. I obsessed over every little thing he said, trying to pick it apart to find something mean or bad or ominous. Something that meant he really didn't like me. But I never found it, and eventually I stopped thinking only about what he was feeling, started thinking about what I was feeling. After six months, I relaxed a little—he had proved to me that it was okay to cut myself a little slack. The next summer, I was actually comfortable enough to go away for a two-week vacation with him. That was when he said he loved me. I said it back, of course—and suddenly things weren't scary at all."

Ruth's main fear was that she would revert to old behavior and drive the guy away. For Amy, a twenty-nine-year-old media planner, it was more the fear that he would spook her. "I had just gotten out of a four-year relationship and was truly enjoying the single life," she says. "I didn't want to get saddled into anything too soon. The last year of my relationship had been extremely stressful; once it had finally ended, I finally got some sleep, got some peace of mind. And it showed—men who had never noticed me before started to pay extra attention. I felt wanted, sexy. I went out on a lot of dates; I felt independent. I was enjoying my space.

"Then I met Anthony. We met at an annual sales meeting in New York. His company was based in Boston (as was mine), and so I was happy to spend the otherwise boring weekend with a fellow Bostonian. We promised to call each other once we got back home. And I fully planned to call him, I had no qualms about it—it was part of my new independence. But he beat me to the punch. He called and asked me to dinner—we went and even kissed a little bit. We ended up going back to my apartment and had amazing sex. He was so passionate, it was almost overwhelming. I told him I'd call him soon and sent him home.

"The next day, he called—even though I had specified that I would do the calling—and invited himself over. I gave in.

I had been thinking about him a lot. But in keeping with the new independence, I didn't want to get attached to a new guy. Still, I figured it couldn't hurt. He came over every night after that for a week. We practically burned through the sheets on my bed. Finally, I said that I needed a rest. He said, 'Okay, let's go to the movies.' I said, 'No, I mean I need a few days apart from you.' He looked hurt, but he left.

"For about an hour, I felt relieved. Then I started wishing he were there. I was getting used to him. I got more and more nervous. I remembered how suffocated I felt with my ex, and I didn't want that to happen again. After a few more months of dating Anthony and feeling more and more like he was a necessity rather than a luxury, I freaked out. I didn't want to lean on someone like that. I told him I needed space. He said, 'You need space, I'll give you Montana,' and walked out the door. My immediate reaction, again, was relief. Then guilt. Then utter loneliness. After a few days, I missed Anthony so much, I felt like it hurt to take a breath. I realized that I had regained my independence at the cost of losing someone whom I loved. I called him. He didn't return my call. I tried again. And again. Finally he agreed to meet me for coffee. We met and decided to try again. I was lucky—I got a chance to realize that you can be independent with a guy as opposed to being dependent on him. For once in my life, I could have my cake and eat it, too."

Speed Demons

As we've already seen, relationships have wildly varying acceleration levels: Every woman marches to the beat of a different heart. Some romances burst open overnight, like poppies. Others bloom in their own sweet time, like the most stubborn of roses. And although we could make an argument for either pace, the fact is, the only speed that really gets you anywhere in love is cruise, minus the control.

There are women — test pilots, astronauts, members of the Star Fleet Command — who can effortlessly travel at the speed of light. Most of us get queasy at the thought of it. Not Louise, a twenty-nine-year-old journalist. "I had just broken up with my ex-jerk, dated a little and hated it," she says. "A friend of mine invited me to a black-tie party with her; she said there would be a lot of available men there. I told her I wasn't looking, that I was sick of going out and hoping that Mr. Right would be there, whoever he might be. She insisted. So I went under duress and started drinking immediately to amuse myself.

"I started talking to a girl that I had known years ago, from summer camp. She took me over to introduce me to her boyfriend, who was standing with a friend of his, Brett. I thought Brett was pretty cute. We all got to chatting and decided to go out for a drink at a nearby bar. At the end of the night, Brett and I traded phone numbers.

"Two days later, Brett called me. It turned out that he lived in Washington — I lived in New York — but that he would be in town again the next week. We went out and had a terrific time. The next weekend, I went to Washington, supposedly to visit a friend but really to see him. Again, we had a wonderful time together. All of a sudden, I decided I really liked him. On the train going home, I wrote in my journal: I'm going to marry this guy. It sounds ridiculous, but something inside me was so certain. It was so right. We saw each other the next three weekends, at which point we said the L-word. Then he moved to New York. In two months, we were living together; in four months, we were engaged. Before the year was out, we were married. For some reason, I never had a single doubt, and neither did he. The relationship had momentum, it just kept moving forward. Still does, by the way."

· · ·

Well, bully for Louise and her perfect little life. Okay, we admit we're a bit staggered by her practically overnight success, but it just proves, once again, that it's worth it to go with the flow. Abbie, a thirty-five-year-old novelist, also went with the flow—albeit one with the speed of continental drift.

"Matthew and I originally met in junior high school," she says. "We had some of the same friends, but we never really hung out together. He said we went on a date once, but I don't remember it. I said we met for drinks once after college, but he didn't remember. Then, ten years after graduating from high school, we both ended up at the wedding of a mutual friend.

"I first saw him in the church. It was after the ceremony, and I was walking out. I remember turning and smiling to the whole group of people he was with. But I was really looking at him, and he at me. It was one of those eye-contact moments. At the reception, we spent a lot of time together, dancing, flirting just the tiniest bit. I woke up the next day and thought, wow, I had such a nice time with him. I didn't think, oh my god, I'm in love—it was more of a little electrical current. I never considered the possibility that Matthew could be it. I just thought he was another guy who could be something.

"He had said after the wedding that we should get together. I didn't know if he meant on a date, or just as old friends. I figured it was the latter. I even considered setting him up with one of my friends, but I decided to hold out for a bit. It was a smart move. He called, we went out—and after that, I had no doubts as to his intentions. We went to dinner and ended up kissing on the street for about an hour.

"We continued to see each other, about once or twice a week. I was very happy, but I certainly wasn't sitting around fantasizing about marrying him or anything. We were both out of heartbreaking relationships and were extremely cautious. Maybe overly cautious, who knows. We weren't even exclusive until a year later, around the time we finally said we loved each other. We took it day by day for months. After two years together, we still only saw each other about three times a week. After three years, we decided to throw caution to the wind and get married. The best part about it all was working things out slowly, but working them out together. I made a concerted effort to keep my romantic expectations down to a realistic level—I figured that way, I wouldn't be disappointed. And Matthew has never disappointed me."

Oh, we could go on and on with these happy beginnings, but time and space don't permit. So we decided to limit ourselves to just a few more stories, the meet-cute kind. Would you believe . . .

- "We met at an AIDS clinic—we were both in the waiting room, waiting to get tested. We got to talking—we joked that if our results were both negative, we'd go out on a date, and then we traded phone numbers. Two weeks later the results were in, and sure enough, they were both negative. We went out to dinner—and kept on going for another two years."
- "I was at a cash machine, getting money. A guy walked in to use the machine next to mine. I looked at him—he was this blond, blue-eyed, all-American type—and I thought, this is the kind of boy I'd like to bring home to my parents. He caught me looking at him and we locked eyes for a good, long moment. Then I left. A week later, I was with my roommates on a Sunday afternoon. I didn't know them very well; I was new to the city. One of them suggested that we hang out at the house of some guys that she knew, who lived right around the corner. We said okay and went over there. Who should answer the door but Mr. All-American

himself. He was going out running, but when he saw me he turned around and sat on the couch. I sat down with him, and we stayed there all afternoon. He called me up a day later and asked me out. He said later that, at the cash machine, he had thought to himself, how could I let this girl go without saying anything?"

- "We met at a party but never exchanged addresses or phone numbers. He told me later that he had really liked me. The next day, he tried to get my phone number but didn't have any luck—I'm unlisted. He was under the impression that I lived in the building where the party was (I didn't), so he wrote a letter to me with that address. About two weeks later, he got the letter back, marked Return to Sender. He said he was really bummed; he thought, I'll never find her. Dejected, he went for a walk and bumped into . . . me. Talk about coincidence."

- "I was running in my second New York City Marathon. Somewhere along First Avenue, I looked over my shoulder and noticed a cute guy running just a few paces behind me. It seemed like he was staring at my ass—not a bad choice since, after fifteen miles, my ass muscles were in peak form. I laughed to myself and kept going. Another half-mile along, I looked again. He was still staring at my ass. He saw me catch him and he blushed—or at least I think he did; it was hard to tell because his face was already bright red from exertion. I slowed down and we fell into pace together. We didn't talk for the next six miles. Then he started to flag. He said he didn't think he was going to make it. I slowed down, too, and tried to psych him up to finish. We crossed the finish line together, practically at a walk. He was so grateful, he asked me to have dinner with him the next night. We ran another marathon together the next year. And now we're thinking of trying out a new kind of marathon—the marriage kind—pretty soon."

- "I'd been doing stand-up comedy for a few months, and I finally felt ready to invite some friends to come and see my act. It was at a comedy club uptown. I was so nervous about my friends being there, I barely noticed the other comics on the line-up. I finally went on and did my act. The crowd loved it—or at least my friends did. They stood up and cheered. It felt great. Then the next comic took the stage. I didn't know who he was, but up there, under the lights, he looked damn good. He had told a few jokes when, suddenly, he stopped. He said, 'I'm sorry, people. I don't think romance is funny, and after watching the girl who went before me, I'm too much in love to do this right now.' He got off the stage and came over to me. The spotlight followed. He asked me out, and the crowd cheered. I said yes, of course. And I kept on saying yes. Even after we got married."

- "I had been looking for a job at a consulting firm for a while. Finally, by networking like crazy, I got an interview with one of the partners at a big company. I went out and bought an interview suit, new shoes, the works. The day of the interview, I showed up and, just my luck, the partner, Mr. Kaplan, had left sick that morning. I was so upset, I swore out loud in front of the receptionist and then wanted to bite my tongue off. I was about to run out when a young guy came around the corner and asked if I was there to see Mr. Kaplan. I said that I was, but that he had gone home sick. The young guy said that he was going to interview me instead. We had spent about a half hour talking about my credentials when he sort of sighed and said, 'The truth is, you really don't have enough experience for this job. We've had applicants with five more years under their belts. But,' and then he paused, 'I think that we should have dinner anyway. I'm really a nice guy, even though you might not think so right now.' He was really nice, so I went. Now we've been living together for six months. I didn't get the job—but I did get the guy."

Which brings us to the last stop on the Heartbreak Express. The final destination. The end of the line. What are you waiting for—*get off, already.*

Yes, dear readers, all the Sturm und Drang has finally reached a conclusion. All the stories have been spun and unspun, all the tales have been . . .

VAL: Wait a minute

. . . told. Laid to rest are the doubts and fears that . . .

VAL: Hold it, hold on a second

. . . haunt the days and nights of the heartbroken. The truth has finally been revealed, and now we can . . .

V: Cut! Cut!

E: Val, do you mind? We were on a roll.

V: Roll, schmoll. I hate when we get all poetic. Besides which, we're not done yet.

E: What do you mean, we're not done yet? We've gone through our whole spectrum of stories. We've exhausted our sources. In less poetic terms. We've shot our wad.

V: Not precisely, my dear Watson. There's just a little more wad left.

E: Meaning?

V: Meaning there's you and Alex. And me and Greg.

E: Oh, Val.

V: Don't you "oh, Val" me. It's our civic duty. It's the right and proper thing to do. And besides, it's my favorite part.

E: Fine. Fine. You first or me?

V: You. No, me. No, you.

E: Indecisive to the last. Okay, here it is. Not quite three months after Jake and I broke up, you and I decided to throw a Christmas party. Remember?

v: Like it was yesterday.

E: We invited everyone and their mother. Unfortunately, everyone and their mother and their mother's mother showed up. It was a mob scene. Two hundred people were crammed into our friend Frank's apartment. Things got broken, the couch caught fire — it was a mess.

v: You and I were running around like chickens with their heads cut off. That is, if a chicken could ever squeeze into the tiny dress you were wearing.

E: Anyway, as the party continued to crash and burn through the night, more and more guests kept showing up. One of them was this guy, Alex, whom I sort of knew through work. I always thought he was cute and interesting — evidently, he returned the compliment — but when we had met in the past, we were both in serious relationships. Someone from our office must have invited him, because I didn't.

v: Me neither.

E: The thing was, he had moved to Chicago a couple of weeks before, so I was surprised to see him. I flirted with him for about five minutes — I didn't have much more time than that, since I was busy checking to see what else was on fire — and in the course of our banter, he said, "You should come out to Chicago." I said, "Oh, I will." He said, "No, I mean it," and I said, "So do I." He said, "You promise?" And I said, "Definitely." And then I walked away. I never thought he'd take me seriously.

v: Of course not. Who would take a girl in a dress like that seriously?

E: Two weeks later, I had gone out on a real clinker of a date, and I woke up the next morning in a foul mood. I was on the phone with my friend Carol, stomping around the apartment, grumbling about how I was bored, how I was in a rut, how I wanted something new and exciting, how I needed an adventure. At that very moment, my call-waiting beeped in. I answered it, and it was . . .

v: Alex.

E: None other. I said, "Can you hold for a minute?" went back to Carol, said, "Carolthere'sthisguyonthephonethatwasat-ourpartywho—nevermindI'llcallyoulater," and returned to Alex.

v: Who said . . . ?

E: Who said, "A couple of weeks ago you made me a prom-ise—do you remember what it was?" Thank god I did, so I could say with a clear conscience, "I remember." And he said, "I was calling to see if you would make good on it."

v: Wow. Elly, he hardly knew ye.

E: I know. I thought about it for a fraction of a second, and then I said, as casually as possible, "Sure."

v: Sure? You said *sure*? Talk about Zen and the art of picking up guys.

E: I told you, I wanted an adventure. So I bought a plane ticket and flew out to Chicago three weeks later. To make a long story longer, we had a great time. Amazing. I didn't see Chicago at all—but I loved the place. He came to New York the next weekend. I went back out the weekend after that. Before I knew what had happened, we were "in-volved." God, I hate that word. And that's that.

v: Except for one little part . . .

E: What part?

v: You know, the L-U-V part. The three-little-words part.

E: Oh, honestly. Okay, we went to Las Vegas for a press junket one weekend, about a month and a half into the whole thing. Las Vegas is, arguably, the armpit of the world, but Alex had a way of making it all seem nicer. Right before I got on the red-eye to come back to New York, he said to me, "Are we falling in love?" And I said, "Maybe . . . I think so . . . I guess." He said, "I hate tiptoeing around it like this. I love you. There. I said it." And I said, "Me, too."

v: You coward—you just couldn't say it, could you? Your mouth just couldn't form the words.

e: Maybe not, but I felt it, which is way more important than saying it. Besides which, three months later, I moved halfway across the country to be with him. If that's not love, what is?

v: True, true. And now you're going to get married and have a nice house with a white picket fence and a whole brood of children and . . .

e: Val, stop projecting. Save it for your own story—which I know you're practically bursting to share.

v: If you insist. Greg and I met at a different party we threw at Frank's.

e: Maybe we should think about throwing parties for a living . . .

v: Maybe we should think of canonizing Frank. Anyway, Frank introduced me to Greg, and I was as attracted to him as I am to doing my taxes.

e: Meaning not at all.

v: I think it was mutual. The next day, I was talking to Frank, and I was complaining that there was no one out there for me. I said, "I'll be alone forever. My life is meaningless."

e: Where have I heard that before?

v: And Frank said, "Well, Val, there was one guy at the party who flipped over you." I asked, "Who?" And Frank said, "His name is Greg."

e: At which point you felt an overwhelming desire to be audited.

v: Nah. I have to admit that the fact that he had it for me bad, suddenly made him look a lot better to me.

e: To me, too.

v: So Greg and I got fixed up and agreed to meet at a bar. I made plans with some friends for later in the night so I could secure a hasty exit. I ended up staying two and a half hours and blowing off my friends, which made me feel a little guilty.

e: Don't worry about it; we didn't miss you at all.

v: Greg turned out to be cute and funny and smart. The thing was, he was so damn cocky. I was confused—why was he so sure of himself when he was supposedly desperate to meet me?

e: Why, indeed?

v: In all fairness, I was pretty cocky that night, too.

e: And you know what happens when two cocky people get together . . .

v: Right. We got together. About four times in a row.

e: That night?

v: No, I mean we went out for the next four consecutive nights—he's good, but he's not Superman. About two months down the road, we were lying in bed one morning and Greg started telling me about how he only goes out with women who chase him first. He said it was because he was shy—he didn't want to risk rejection. I said, "Not this time, Pepe Le Pew." He said, "No, this time too."

e: Do I smell a skunk?

v: I said, "Look. Frank told me you were bursting your Levis to date me." Greg said, "*Au contraire, petit chat.* He said you were champing at the bit to date me." Needless to say, I hated the horse analogy.

e: Who wouldn't?

v: But after we recovered from realizing we'd been hood-winked, we managed to forge ahead. About four months later, we were having sex and he said, "I think I love you."

e: Which would've made any normal girl happy, but then again, you've never disappointed us with your normality.

v: I was upset. He *thought* he loved me? *Thought?* Why didn't he know? *I* knew.

e: I think you were overreacting. No, I know you were.

v: Well, after three days of you singing that Partridge Family song in my face, over and over, I realized I was overreacting, too.

e: Always glad to be of service.

v: A few weeks later, again in bed, he said out of the blue, "You know how I feel about you, don't you?" And I said, "I *think* I do."

e: So good at letting go . . .

v: He said, "I love you." And I said, "I love you, too—I just want you to be happy."

e: You mean sappy. I'm going to be sick.

v: What can I say? I'm a hopeless romantic. So was he, it turned out. He proposed after ten months. I accepted, of course. I couldn't believe it.

e: *You* couldn't believe it . . .

v: I had always thought I'd be the last of all my friends to tie the knot. But as it turns out, I'm one of the first. And you know what? It's not half as scary as I thought it would be.

e: It never is.

And that's all we wrote. We were going to wrap up by saying we lived happily ever after—but that would be too predictable. Instead, we'll settle for: So far, so good. Which really isn't settling at all.

Photo by Marshall Sella

About the Authors

VAL FRANKEL attended Dartmouth College, worked at *New York Woman* magazine, and is the author of the Wanda Mallory Mystery Series (including *Murder On Wheels* and *Prime Time for Murder*). ELLEN TIEN attended Vassar College and was co-founder and editor-in-chief of *Metro* magazine, a New York City monthly. They met at *Mademoiselle* magazine, where they began writing together. Val is currently an editor at *Mademoiselle*; Ellen is a senior editor at *Cosmopolitan* magazine. They both live and work in New York City.